Advertising
on Trial

Advertising on Trial

Managing your Agency for Effective Results

JIM RING

FINANCIAL TIMES

PITMAN PUBLISHING

Pitman Publishing
128 Long Acre, London WC2E 9AN

A Division of Longman Group UK Limited

First published in 1993

© Jim Ring 1993

A CIP catalogue record for this book can be obtained from the
British Library.

ISBN 0 273 03970 9

Photoset in Linotron Times Roman by
Northern Phototypesetting Co. Ltd, Bolton
Printed and bound in Great Britain by
Biddles Ltd, Guildford and King's Lynn

It is always an advantage not to have received a sound commercial education.

OSCAR WILDE
The Portrait of Mr W. H.

In real terms, world advertising expenditure per person has doubled since the 1950s. In this sense, the growth of crime is not surprising.

DAVID NICHOLSON-LORD
The Independent, 3 January 1993

For Stella Ring

CONTENTS

ACKNOWLEDGEMENTS

A number of people have greatly helped me with this book.

Firstly my employers, Wight Collins Rutherford Scott, who have been quite indulgent at a time at which the agency has been busy. I have the company's deputy chairman Mike Manwaring to thank particularly here, even though naturally I would no more expect him to agree with every single opinion in the book than I would WCRS itself, or the Queen.

Two people read the whole text and made a number of suggestions. These were Alan Page of Harari Page and Ian Croll of Arc Advertising. Others have commented on individual chapters: from WCRS Richard Swaab, Justin Bairamian, John Thorpe and Simon Toaldo; from Payne/Stracey Andrew Stracey; and Linnet Macintyre and Tony Finnegan, formerly of TBWA. Sophie McLaughlin of WCRS devised some of the diagrams.

A series of companies and organisations have kindly provided case-histories and other documentary material. They are Benetton(UK)Ltd; Fuji Photo Film(UK)Ltd and Howell Henry Chaldecott Lury; the Department of Health; Vin & Sprit and TBWA; Bass Brewers Ltd and WCRS; and the Incorporated Society of British Advertisers.

Others have been generous enough to let me use their advertising as illustrations of various points: the Prudential Assurance Company Ltd, Gallaher Tobacco (UK) Ltd, Mills & Allen Ltd, Courage Ltd, Lynx (Helping Abused Animals) Ltd, Crookes Healthcare Ltd, and Haagen-Dazs(UK) Ltd.

I also have to thank J. Walter Thompson, the Henley Centre, Payne/Stracey and NTC Publications for some of the figures.

Finally, those who did the real work. Kate Faire loaded most of the work on to the machine provided by WCRS; Jackie Darvell did the detail.

PART ONE

During the eighties advertising became all about making beautiful ads. It was very indulgent and sophisticated, but there was no proof that these ads were selling more of the client's products. In a recession the client couldn't care less about winning all these advertising awards; he wants to shift his stock.

PAUL BAINSFAIR
Bainsfair Sharkey Trott

PRELUDE:
NIGHTMARE ON
MADISON AVENUE
Advertising in recession

Only half my advertising works. The trouble is I don't know which half.
LORD LEVERHULME

*The recession · impact on marketing and advertising people worldwide ·
doing more for less · pressure to show that advertising works · need to make
advertising work better · lack of help in doing so · purpose of the book ·
its argument · the empirical approach to advertising · success for the reader
unavoidable*

If you work in the marketing or advertising businesses, the last three or four
years may well have been the toughest of your professional life.

The recession has been bad enough. It's been longer, deeper and more
severe than anticipated by even the most pessimistic, hitting the industrialised nations as hard as anything else for thirty years. In Britain it meant
in 1991 alone that while gross domestic product (GDP) stooped, interest
rates remained punitively high, consumer spending on almost everything
other than staples fell, more than half a million people lost their jobs, and
some 75,000 homes were repossessed. Every single business in the country
was affected, some – the vehicle and building trades – finding themselves 30
per cent down. And one in forty-three of the others simply failed to make it
through the year. This is merely an instance. A lot of people – a lot of
companies – in a lot of countries have suffered. Of course, marketing people
are scarcely unique in this, but of all those still in employment, they often
feel particularly under pressure. Seen as they are to spearhead efforts to
support the bottom line, they suppose themselves to be under close enough
scrutiny from their colleagues, let alone their bosses. Moreover, as many
companies continue to fund their marketing activities directly as opposed to
indirectly from sales, they are also faced with the very considerable problem

of increasingly being asked to do their ever more difficult jobs with smaller and smaller budgets. They have been told that less must be more.

And yet, alongside these psychological and financial imperatives lies an almost paradoxical rise in the perceived importance of the marketing process. The notion that companies should be producing services and goods that their customers want, as opposed to merely what it is convenient for them to provide, is not a new one. Still, it's scarcely unfair to say that it has been only over the past ten or fifteen years with the likes of McDonalds, Mars, Procter & Gamble, Sony and British Airways, that many companies seem to have put the idea intentionally rather than fortuitously into practice. The consequences have been that marketing activities have at last begun to be given the attention they – arguably – deserve by management outside the discipline itself, that these people have acquired a little learning about the subject, and that as well as finding their way on to the balance-sheet, a few brands have actually begun to be genuinely marketed. All these things have pleasingly increased the status of marketing people, while simultaneously adding to their burden. Marketing is increasingly regarded as that which it is not: a universal panacea.

With approximately half of most marketing budgets being spent on advertising, there's some truth in saying that the buck then stops with the ad-man. It is certainly true that if the 1980s was the decade in which advertising never had it so good, the new decade has so far seen the business enduring its worst downturn for a generation. In 1991 worldwide ad spending fell – by 2.9 per cent – for the first time in twenty years. The huge North American market was down 5.9 per cent, Europe by 2.0 per cent, and only the Far East showed growth – and this with severe depression in Australia and New Zealand.

All this is, of course, partly a direct consequence of recession, but there is also evidence of more deep-seated change which won't simply be waived away as, and when, economic prospects brighten. The fact is that while the recession has naturally caused advertisers to review, reconsider and often cut their budgets – as I write Britain's biggest bank has just halved its advertising budget – it has also made them examine more closely than ever before the economics of advertising. And, generally, in the absence of concrete, convincing and quantitative evidence to the contrary, those economics have been found wanting. At a time at which enthusiasm to account for every dollar spent is naturally high, it is simply not clear enough to many advertisers exactly what they're getting for the large sums of money they are spending, exactly what return they're seeing on their investment. Advertising – ever a business to excite the suspicions of the sceptic – is, as a consequence, more than ever before on trial and, as has been written of the last great advertising depression in the mid 1970s, is 'justifiably expected to produce convincing evidence in its own defence'. Thus advertisers almost everywhere take the view of one of their leaders quoted in the British trade magazine *Campaign*: 'We want better strategies, better targeting, better creativity, better media placement, better thinking. We aim to ensure we get agencies' best people on our business and then ensure they are motivated to work their butts off, producing outstanding work for us.'

Now, while none of this should or is intended to elicit sympathy for a thoroughly tough business, it does mean that many of those advertising people still in work are facing precisely the same problems as their clients: how to do more with less. And that's something which seems likely to continue for some time yet.

If this is all in itself sufficiently trying, a number of other things have made the production of effective advertising particularly difficult. Some of these are a direct consequence of recession: the controversy over production costs, and the disinclination to take the sort of risks that are ironically often the essence of good advertising. Other events would have happened irrespective of local or global economic conditions: the dramatic demographic changes facing much of the west; the burgeoning power of the retailer; the growing appreciation of the need for advertising to work in close conjunction with the other ways in which brands communicate themselves ranging from sponsorship to packaging; the changing needs and desires of consumers; the rise of sponsorship; the fragmentation of media coupled with the consolidation of media buying and ownership; the increasingly onerous legal restrictions on advertising. And, of course, for some companies there is the new challenge of advertising abroad. Together with the recession, it is these matters which have forced many of those responsible for advertising to revisit Lord Leverhulme's commonplace that 'Only half my advertising works. The trouble is I don't know which half. 'Because now more than ever before, the pressure is on to increase the proportion of advertising that works.

It is not terribly surprising that, at the moment, help for those – mainly on the marketing but also on the advertising side of the fence – who want or need to do just that is far from freely available. Generally, advertisers and their agencies have been far too busy simply coping with these circumstances to wish to talk or write about them, while those that have succeeded in keeping their heads above water are often understandably anxious to keep the secrets of their success to themselves. This means that while conferences and seminars may provide some useful information, the books currently available on advertising and how to do it really don't. This is of course mainly because the limited number that are on the shelves were generally drafted before the recession and inevitably ignore subsequent events. But they also tend to treat the process of producing advertising with too much respect. Advertising is a cavalier business that can ride roughshod over those prepared to let it do so, foisting indifferent material on its clients and occasionally charging grossly for so doing. To give the impression that the work agencies produce is invariably of the highest quality, deeply-considered and remarkable value for money is neither true nor likely to help those on the client side who are ultimately responsible. This book accordingly takes the opportunity both to bring the advertising scene up to date, and to treat it more sceptically than is normally the case for what is intended to be an entirely practical guide.

Its argument is that – not surprisingly – there's no simple, single way of improving advertising productivity – by which is meant return on advertising investment. Rather that the rapidity of changes in the advertising environment mean that it's necessary to re-examine every aspect of the contemporary advertising process, and achieve incremental improvements in each and every one.

To do this, the book tells the whole story of the advertising process, starting by looking at advertising in the broader context of 'integrated' or total communications marketing. It then looks at everything from hiring an agency, the setting of advertising objectives, developing a strategy, creative work and media proposals, to the assessment of whether and how well the creativity has actually worked, culminating in the natural process of firing the agency and starting all over again. And, rather than merely rehearsing received wisdom, it looks critically at the way marketing departments and advertising agencies actually, rather than theoretically, develop advertising, using examples of best practice to illustrate exactly how these should and can be improved. It also looks at the problems of advertising in foreign markets, and concludes with a section which modestly sets out a prescription for agencies in the 1990s. Ultimately, this traces the poverty of the current advertising scene to the nature of the relationship between agencies and their clients, and argues that the best way of getting better advertising lies partly in improving this, and partly in adopting a more empirical approach to the whole advertising process. This means being more open-minded as to what ads *may* influence the consumer, and far more energetic in discovering which ones actually *have*.

While very far from the last word on advertising – not expected to be written quite yet – *Advertising on Trial* is nevertheless a cornucopia of strategies and devices, tactics and ploys that advertising managers beginning their careers may use to help them get the best out of the agency doing their advertising. As a whole it is therefore intended to contribute in the most specific and concrete ways possible to making the next two or three years more fulfilling and rewarding for marketing (and advertising) people than the last, thus sharing with '*Inlaws and Outlaws*' – one of Professor C. Northcote Parkinson's various works of genius – the intention of making success for the reader 'practically unavoidable'.

I THE SEA OF TROUBLES
Total communications planning

'Might have been made for you,' said Mr Levy.
'But I don't know a word of German, I've had no experience, I've got no testimonials, and I don't play cricket.'
'It doesn't do to be too modest,' said Mr Levy. 'It's wonderful what one can teach if one tries. Why, only last term we sent a man who had never been in a laboratory in his life as Senior Science Master to one of our leading public schools. He came wanting to do private coaching in music. He's doing very well I believe. Besides, Dr Fagan can't expect all that for the salary he's offering.'

EVELYN WAUGH
Decline and Fall

The unhappy marketer · pressure to act · need to stop and consider · brand planning and the brand audit · total communication auditing – what is a brand? · how to conduct the audit · setting communication objectives · qualities of different forms of communication · developing a communication strategy · establishing the need for advertising

Settling into a new job is rarely a pleasant process. The position is advertised in the national press and the company has a good reputation for marketing; it's billed as a position of some potential and would appear to be a good second job; the candidates are many, their qualifications impressive, and all of them seem to imagine it to be the next step in an exciting marketing career. The interview is exacting and the ultimate offer generous: an attractive hike in salary comes for the first time with a car, relocation expenses, a surprisingly spacious office, and the congratulatory letters from friends and colleagues that mark such appointments. A glorious future seems assured in which there seems to be a good chance of emulating John Sculley's odyssey from Pepsi to Apple, or Ernest Saunders' happier achievements at Guinness.

Yet you may well feel yourself in the first days rather like the late Robert Maxwell – pitched into a sea of troubles. By definition few brands are leaders and the managers of those that are sometimes less sanguine than might be imagined. They are often paranoid about losing their number one spot and suffering from pressure on margins, problems with supply, together with Machiavellian internal politics over who is to take credit for the success, or worrying themselves to death over where to go next. Brands and their owners not enjoying the position of leader then face the usual problems to which number twos and below are heir: erosion by own-label, inconsistent product performance, competitive launches, sabotage by animal rights activists, disastrous line-extensions, sales promotions grossly compromising positioning, and sales-forces disgruntled because their saloons have just been replaced by hatchbacks. Couple this with the general effects of recession, something approaching a crisis in the marketers' main tool of advertising, and the pressures to present plans to the marketing director in six weeks, and the euphoria of the appointment may evaporate. Something must be done at once.

However, this is more debatable than might at first appear. Marketers and their colleagues in other management disciplines subscribe more frequently these days to the notion of marketing and assume that brands must therefore be managed; and it follows that there should be people around called brand managers, marketing managers and the like. Yet the extent to which managers actually manage brands is open to question. For, given that brand management is essentially about the manipulation of the marketing mix – conventionally the product, its price, its promotion and its distribution – in many situations the scope for manoeuvre is limited:

1 the *product* is set in stone, or so fiercely guarded by R and D, product management or the head brewer to mean that nothing you can do or your customers can say will change it;
2 *price* seems to be a conspiracy between retailers, trade marketing and the company's financial management;
3 *distribution* is simply whatever the sales department can manage, irrespective of marketing's most sophisticated notions of targeting;
4 *the advertising* is a famous and long-running campaign, jealously protected by the agency, apparently more for the purposes of its own promotion than that of your brand.

It follows that although marketing departments are certainly under considerable pressures to be seen to be doing something, the possibilities – and dangers – of actually doing just that are perhaps slightly less real. Short of reformulating the product along the lines of the 'new Coke' débâcle, or contaminating it in the manner of Perrier's spectacular 1989 benzine disaster, relatively little you can do as manager in the first weeks or months of your appointment can dramatically affect the brand. Moreover, it's probably worth remarking that this may well be all to the good. The enthusiasm of new brooms to be seen to make their mark is understandable and well documented. Similarly familiar is the failure of short-term, ill-considered, ill-conceived tampering with brands. Brand management is, in fact, in many if not the majority cases a long-term business that requires the incremental adjustment of brand image – occasionally even brand reality – to changing public tastes. Largely because of the ways in which companies are managed, there is often enormous pressure on line managers to be seen to be doing something. Yet, the best piece of brand management, at least at first, is invariably to stop, to look and to listen.

WHERE AM I?

Still, it has to be accepted that it is likely that attempts in due course will have to be made at least to try to do something with the brand – a something that may well include advertising. The question is what. This is supposedly the *raison d'être* of brand management, and most companies of any size and competence have established disciplines to help you arrive at reasonable answers to the question. In the context of what is the best starting-point for producing good advertising – *setting the job for advertising in the larger context of a total communication strategy* – it is enough to say here that six stages are normally used to establish what usually takes the form of the annual brand plan.

1 A general look at the *social and economic factors* likely to affect future brand performance: on a brand of ethnic foods that might include the increased incidence of foreign travel, and the growth of a country's ethnic community; on a newspaper the explosion of the electronic media like video and satellite TV, and the standards of reading in schools.
2 The assessment of the brand's *current business status*, typically in terms of volume, margins and contribution to the bottom line.
3 The *setting of business goals*, normally using the same sort of variable.
4 The *setting of marketing objectives* derived from the business goals, usually by way of distribution, consumer penetration and market share.
5 The *development of marketing strategies* appropriate to these goals: product reformulations, distribution drives, sales promotions, advertising etc.
6 Plans for the *execution of these strategies* within a given budget and against a set timetable.

Most people in marketing or advertising will equally be more than aware of the limitations of such planning, notably the problems of reconciling attractive projections to less satisfactory reality, and the inclination of companies to set marketing budgets unrelated to the scope or scale of the marketing job to be done. But the real problem from the point of view of communication planning lies in the emphasis placed on financial performance to an extent irrespective of the status of the brand. This is important because, however plausible the projected growth in volume and share may appear, in the absence of significant improvements in the product, its pricing or distribution, these aren't likely to be achieved unless:

- the sentiments of existing consumers towards the brand are changed, increasing frequency of purchase;
- the number of consumers who share favourable feelings towards the brand are increased – increasing penetration.

And, not unnaturally, these changes are more likely to be achieved if the *current status of the brand in the eyes of the consumer* – as opposed to the company's balance-sheets – is known. It follows that the first step in the business of communication planning is to ensure that the standing of the brand *is* exactly known. Generally, as a manager of a decent-sized brand you will know:

- total market size and trends;
- your own market share, volumes and brand awareness;
- who buys the brand;
- competitive market share and volumes;
- distribution patterns;
- contributions of your own brand.

What you usually need to know more precisely is what existing and potential consumers think and feel about the brand at that moment, particularly *why* the brand is bought. Brand, product and line profiles are relatively easily obtainable and come in the comforting form of figures; qualitative, sometimes quantitative, information on consumer motivation is inevitably softer and more a matter of opinion and interpretation than fact – but it is ultimately more important. The reason *why* people buy something is the key to understanding how they may be persuaded to buy more; and equally why in certain – sometimes predictable – future circumstances they may well buy less.

Although the precise issues depend on product sector – whether the brand is a newspaper, a bicycle or a nappy – broadly the need is to know the following.

1 *Why people generally buy products in the sector*. This clearly means looking at underlying motivation. Alcohol consumption is more

concerned with conviviality and sociability than with getting drunk; people visit bars to consume other people as much as to drink. Similarly, newspapers purport to peddle news, but in practice both the serious and more popular titles provide what Rupert Murdoch of News International once acutely, if somewhat inelegantly, called 'infotainment'.

2 *Why given brands are bought as opposed to alternatives.* Are there significant product differences or is imagery all? Denim jeans are in reality commodities in which clever marketing means that imagery plays the biggest part in influencing brand choice. However, with washing-machines more functional qualities prevail.

3 *What decision-making process customers go through to arrive at the choice of a brand* – and therefore how those choices can be influenced. Some buying is very much a question of custom: some quite rational and carefully planned; some largely impulsive.

4 Whether the brand suffers from any particular *barriers which discourage purchase*. For instance, is it an ageing brand in a youth-oriented market? Or is it something priced at a premium with no obvious product superiority, under threat from cheaper brands?

5 Whether it has any *assets crucial to protect*. Certain makes of car have reputations very significantly at odds with the realities of their perform-ance, and much the same could be said of some cosmetics. Generally, this is the sort of illusion it is wise to maintain.

6 Finally, what is the claimed *propensity to purchase,* is it changing and how does that differ from the competition? This is a good way of summarising the absolute and relative appeals of a brand, and can be related with a certain degree of accuracy to actual purchasing behaviour.

This all comprises something that in a cost-conscious age can be called a *brand audit*.

If you are working on a large brand, getting this information will be relatively straightforward, even though there will be resistance at certain levels to spending on research to discover it.

(This resistance is a paradox. Companies committed to spending annually very large sums of money on advertising and marketing are reluctant to spend a tiny fraction of that figure on establishing in the first instance how that money should be spent, and ensuring in the second instance that it's been well spent. The rule of thumb for advertising *production* budgets is 10 per cent of total. A similar figure should be allotted to research. In reality, a typical figure is about a tenth of that.)

With smaller brands it will be less easy to find the sort of sums necessary to set up the qualitative and sometimes quantitative consumer research that will provide such information. In these circumstances the combination of a small-scale qualitative study and a complementary study on one of the various syndicated quantitative surveys available will provide the necessary information, the idea being that the themes identified in the first are quantified in the second. The speed of change of most markets means that these data have to be updated at least annually.

WHAT AM I SAYING?

A brand audit is useful because it gives you a proper fix on where the brand currently stands. This is likely, in turn, to give some insights into how easy or difficult it is going to be to improve what people think and feel about the brand, and therefore how realistic are the marketing and ultimately business objectives that have been set for it. However, what it obviously doesn't do is give very much sense as to how – in communication as opposed to broader marketing terms – these things might actually be achieved. The next job in communication planning is accordingly to do a *total communications audit*. Together with the brand audit this is an important process in establishing the most cost-effective way of protecting and enhancing the status of a brand, and ultimately its sales. However, this perhaps begs the question, what is a brand?

Now, while a product is something that can be manufactured on a production-line, carted around the country in 32-ton trucks and placed lovingly on supermarket shelves, a brand can be quite usefully defined as *an idea in the mind of the consumer*. This distinction between an object and a notion is important because it raises the issue of faith. Marketing is, among other things, about encouraging, persuading and cajoling consumers to buy, and this means them parting with their money. Most people, not very surprisingly, approach the business of giving someone money in exchange for something else with a healthy degree of scepticism, uncertainty and doubt. An unbranded tin of cola on the corner-shop's shelves is just a product. A can of Coke is a brand because it possesses the power of reassuring shoppers that their money is well spent. A brand is thus in the first place the idea in the mind of the consumer that the product the brand represents or symbolises is good. It gives consumers something of very considerable value: faith in the product. Then, beyond such fairly functional reassurance, most brands also possess intangible benefits that can be highly influential in persuading consumers to buy. In this sense, to buy a Jaguar is less to possess a car than to participate in British motor-racing history; to buy a packet of a certain washing-powder is to become the embodiment of the caring mother; to fork out a couple of dollars for a packet of Marlboro to embrace the American frontier spirit; to buy a Rolls-Royce is to acquire prestige. It is for these reasons that brands usually command prices significantly above largely comparable products, why they're now highly valued by companies, and why looking after a brand is, in certain respects, an important job. It's also why finding out what each part of the brand presentation is contributing to the brand image is an important part of communication planning.

This is the *total communication audit*. It is based on the idea originated in the 1960s in the US that there are all sorts of things outside your control as marketer – ranging from competitive activity to the passage of time – that affect what people feel about brands. Yet equally there is not just a single element, but a number of them within the marketers' control. In the past, when thinking about brand messages, managers of brands have tended to concern themselves with the most obvious, glamorous and expensive part of the communication package, the advertising. The idea of total communications or integrated marketing is that it takes into account two facts:

- that there's often much more to brand communications than advertising;
- that for the communication to work as effectively as possible, each element should either duplicate or complement the other.

The idea of the communication audit then, is simply to find out in what ways

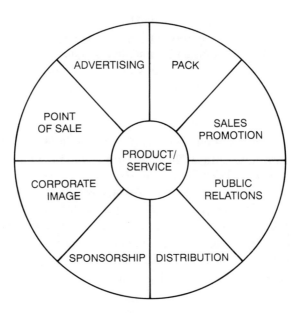

Figure 1.1 What's in a brand?

the elements that you *can* control are affecting what people think and feel about the brand, and specifically whether they're working with or against each other.

Actually producing this information can be done in a number of ways. You can do it yourself, use your customers to help you, or pay a consultant quite a lot of money to do it on your behalf. Doing it yourself is in fact an essential preliminary to all three methods. It simply involves physically assembling every single piece of material produced for, expressive of, or associated with a brand. Naturally, this material will vary from brand to brand, and sector to sector, but covers everything from the most expensive television commercial to the cheapest piece of point-of-sale. For instance, on a beer brand you might have to look at:

- TV advertising;
- press and poster advertising;
- radio advertising;
- the bar front, countermount or dispense unit;
- on-trade promotional material (beer mats, towels and ash-trays etc.)
- sales promotional material;
- vehicle livery;
- brand logo.

Having got all this material together, you are likely to be struck by its diversity. To an extent this is entirely appropriate because you have in front of you various ways of expressing the brand in different environments. However, what is necessary is some degree of coherence and convergence by way of what the material:

- says about the brand; and
- expresses that thought.

The essence of total communication planning is that if this isn't the case the communication will be diffuse, the consumer confused and the marketing budget wasted. Or, to put it the other way round, if the communication package is properly integrated with a fair degree of consistency of theme and expression – utter uniformity can be bland – the sum of its parts will be considerably greater than the whole.

The problem with this way of approaching the process is that it focuses more on what experienced marketers feel about the brand that is their meal-ticket, than on the only thing that really matters: what their customers feel. So it's often worth doing some consumer research to ensure that your own instincts accord with the public's feelings. It is sensible for this to be included as part of the brand auditing process described above, enabling you to hone your understanding of the relationship between what consumers are saying about the brand and what the brand is saying about itself.

The final option is to wash your hands of the whole business and call in outside consultants to do the job. In most marketing departments with adequate personnel resources this is probably unnecessary. Conducting the audit really requires more hard work and common sense than specialised talents or experience, and is a good way of focusing your mind on what the brand stands for and what is being said about it. However, design companies, advertising agencies and marketing consultants are increasingly offering total communication audit services. It's worth seeing what these people have to say and making a decision based on the complexity of the job, your company's resources and the cost of the consultancy.

Unless your brand has been exceptionally well managed you're likely to find as the result of the audit a degree of incoherence both between what is being said about the brand and how it is being said. And this in turn will provide some more ideas as to why the brand is in the shape it's in, and what needs to be done to redress the situation.

WHERE AM I GOING AND WHAT SHOULD I BE SAYING?

If in business circles reason and logic prevailed, your next step would be to set realistic objectives for the brand, based on a thorough knowledge of its existing position – in the eyes of its consumers. In practice this is relatively rare. The commanding principle of most companies that take brands reasonably seriously is likely to be their shareholders' profit expectations, and these in turn are likely to be imposed willy-nilly throughout the firm. So what you're likely to be faced with is, on the one hand, a doubtless far from reassuring health check on the state of the brand and, on the other, some doubtless outrageously ambitious sales and margin objectives set by the management for the upcoming year. It then becomes your job not only to reconcile these two matters, but also to do so within a marketing budget that is imposed from above rather than allocated according to the scale of the marketing task. Still, somehow or other, in the same way as the mortgage has to be paid, the job must be done; and you have to hand the conventional tools of product, price and distribution to help you do it. You also have the tool of communication, or *what is said about the brand*. Now, as this is a book about communication, let's assume a situation – by no means uncommon – in which your hands are largely tied on the issues of product, price and distribution, and the one club in the bag is that of communication. If that is the case, instead of achieving the brand's financial objectives by – say – doubling the number of outlets in which it is available, radically improving the product or halving its price, the job has to be done by significantly improving what people think and feel about an existing brand, without actually changing the thing itself at all.

The particular way in which this is done will of course depend on the nature of the product sector, and the strengths and weaknesses of the particular brand. For instance, if the brand is scarcely known, then simply increasing brand *awareness* almost invariably improves people's opinions about the brand because, by definition, it becomes less of an unknown quantity and – if advertising is used to increase awareness – is accorded the status associated with an advertised product. Equally, if everyone ever likely to buy the brand already knows about it, then the job has to be to say something relevant and true about it that is likely to raise its status. This issue of strategy is relatively complex, and is discussed at length in Chapter 5. In order to pursue the communication planning argument, it's enough here to instance the case of the beer.

CASE HISTORY 1
A Summary Brand Audit

QUESTION	ANSWER
1 Why do people buy beer?	*Like all alcohol, beer helps people socialise and relax. It's a cold and refreshing drink.*
2 Why do people buy particular brands?	*Among standard (as opposed to premium) beers, real product differences are small. Assuming all were equally widely available, choice would be based on the perceived personality or image of the brand.*
3 What is the decision-making process associated with choosing a particular brand?	*Beer is a cheap, ill-differentiated product. Accordingly, purchasing is largely impulsive as opposed to considered. Good packaging and the bar countermount are therefore important in prompting purchase. Advertising is also important in providing a point of difference.*

4 Does the brand suffer from any weaknesses?	*In a market in which imagery is important, your brand lacks the modern and fashionable image of younger brands.*
5 What strengths does it have?	*It's a good product, which once it's sampled commands loyalty.*
6 Who's says they're going to buy it in the future?	*Existing buyers, not young turks.*

The main weakness identified was not brand awareness or product quality, but in the perception that the brand was old-fashioned and out of date. So the solution might be to reposition the brand as a 'classic', and perhaps support that claim with some facts about product superiority. The substance of the communication would then be that the brand has been around so long because the product is so good. From such an argument would then stem specific *communication objectives* which support the main requirement to improve people's perceptions of the brand. On the beer these could be:

1 to exploit consumer knowledge of the brand's longevity by repositioning it as a classic brand that has stood the test of time;
2 to justify this claim by creating consumer awareness that – say – a cold filtration process is used to prepare the product, which gives the beer a uniquely clean taste.

HOW AM I GOING TO SAY IT?

Setting such objectives completes the third stage in the communication planning process, and it now merely remains to decide the best ways of achieving them.

This process – formally the development of a communication strategy – might seem simple enough, but the evidence clearly observable to anyone in the advertising or marketing worlds who keeps their eyes open has to be that in practice it is not. This is partly because there are quite a lot of ways of getting messages across, partly because that range seems to increase daily, partly because some of them are intrinsically more effective than others, and partly because some are intrinsically more appropriate ways of achieving particular communication goals.

For instance, television is a highly intrusive medium that can raise brand awareness very rapidly and give the brand the considerable status of one that is advertised on TV. For a mass-market brand with a large budget available and a name that is little known by the public, it follows that television advertising is an attractive route to investigate. Conversely, television in most countries is very much a mass-market domestic medium. So if it has status, it has little cachet. Accordingly, if you have a niche brand operating on low volumes but high margins, the cult of exclusivity which may well be your objective could be seriously damaged by using TV advertising. Consumers against whom your product is targeted may well wish to believe that they have discovered the brand themselves. It thus follows that PR activity aimed at getting editorial coverage in appropriate 'style' magazines might be a far more appropriate way of spending the communication budget.

The principle then is that the means of communication must be chosen with care to suit the brand, its personality and its problems. Those means of communication, their qualities, strengths and weaknesses are as follows.

Advertising

This is a highly cost-effective way of reaching very large numbers of people and communicating fairly simple messages; and it can also confer considerable status on a brand. The downside is that the capital costs involved – particularly on television – are high, and the precise message it communicates is normally forgotten quite quickly. Of the various forms it's enough here to say that:

1 TV is a highly efficient and rapid way of raising brand awareness and conveying brand image or personality.
2 Cinema has a greater impact than television because of the relatively special nature of the occasion – going to see a film – and the darkened auditorium. However, in many countries relatively few people go to the cinema, and those who do are mainly young.
3 Press is a versatile medium, but is particularly suited to more complicated messages that are intended to inform and explain.
4 Posters can only communicate very simple ideas, either visually or verbally.
5 Radio is a cheap way of reaching quite specific target groups. It can be a highly effective secondary medium, but it entirely lacks the authority of TV.

Packaging

For obvious reasons far more the embodiment of the brand or product than advertising, and intrinsic to it rather than added on – the Gitanes cigarette packet *is* the brand – in the sense of by far the most important and memorable expression of the brand's identity. Packaging until recently was neglected as a way of establishing or manipulating brand imagery. Repackaging milk – out of a bottle into a soft drink presentation – has done a lot for its imagery and, apparently, sales.

Sales promotion

Conventionally shunned by advertising agencies as being beneath their notice, sales promotions can contribute significantly and valuably to a brand's marketing mix and image as opposed to denigrating it. Definable as an offer (two for the price of one, a chance to win a holiday etc.), a promotion which reflects or complements the brand personality can raise its awareness, provide a short-term boost to sales and add something to the brand's image. British Airways' efforts to kick-start the air-travel market after the Gulf War with an offer of free flights on all its routes exemplifies a promotion that combined a sales effect with a positive impact on image. It also provided BA with a valuable database of people seriously interested in flying.

Direct marketing

This is a technique to get prospects to raise their hands and say 'I'm interested, tell me more'. It then follows through the purchase cycle to engender loyalty. It has the advantage of strict accountability and relatively low capital costs. Conversely, it accords the brand little of the status of TV ads, therefore while it is more than capable of affecting short-term awareness and sales, it generally does little for brand imagery and the longer term status of the brand.

Sponsorship

Sponsorship is a marketing tool the use of which has mushroomed over the past ten years as companies have seen the advantages of associating themselves with activities generally outside the commercial sphere. It is also attractive because it avoids using the increasingly regulated advertising medium. However, it has its limitations. It is generally slow (years rather than months) in its impact, it tends to affect awareness more than imagery, and it's not entirely unfair to say that it scarcely works at all unless it is heavily merchandised. The rule of thumb is that for every pound spent on sponsorship, three should be spent making the target aware of the association. It is also often difficult to isolate the effect of sponsorship on imagery. The long-standing Philip Morris Marlboro association with the McLaren Formula 1 motor-racing team nevertheless shows how well the medium can work, while Nike can scarcely have been displeased when their standard-bearer Andre Agassi was seen by 150 million people worldwide winning the 1992 Wimbledon tennis championship.

Sponsorship of television programmes is a fairly new and interesting area, worth examining, Sony in the UK breaking new ground with their work on the Rugby World Cup. The general sponsorship rule – that the sponsorship has to be merchandised – applies very much here.

Public relations

Might perhaps be more accurately termed media relations in so far as the business acknowledges and seeks to exploit the extent to which consumers are influenced by nominally impartial press, TV and radio editorial coverage. Useful for handling relationships with targets as variable as the media it employs, it's surprising how many brands and brand owners still neglect the discipline. By its nature public relations will do relatively little for brand awareness, but can certainly help over a period of time in establishing understanding between a manufacturer and its public.

Corporate image

Again, corporate image was until recently a neglected aspect of the public's relationship with a brand, but it is still a significant one. Although with some companies the body corporate and the brand will be one and the same thing, behind brands like Shredded Wheat, Michelob and Ariel lie large companies – sometimes large individuals – that themselves have an image. And that image can influence the choice of sub-brand.

Price

Normally distinguished in the marketing mix from communication, price is in fact one of the most powerful means of communicating to consumers the value of a brand. As such, price and its manipulation has a profound effect

Medium	Awareness	Imagery	Capital cost	Speed
Advertising	✓ ✓	✓ ✓ ✓	X X X	✓ ✓ ✓
Packaging	✓	✓	X	✓
Sales promotion	✓ ✓	✓	X	✓ ✓
Direct marketing	✓ ✓	✓	X X	✓
Sponsorship	✓	✓ ✓	X X	✓
Public relations	✓	✓	X	✓
Corporate image	✓	✓	X	✓
Price	– – – –	✓ ✓	– – – –	✓
Distribution	✓	✓	X	✓

Figure 1.2 Getting the message across

on brand imagery and can be used as much for that purpose as for more obvious functional reasons.

Distribution

Similarly, distribution is not normally regarded as a means of communication. In fact, brands take colour from their surroundings and achieving appropriate distribution is an important way of saying something about a brand that is often crucial to its success: you wouldn't expect to find a Rolex, or at least a real one, in a cheap jewellery shop. An issue of imagery by association, simply seeing a product on the shelves clearly also creates or reinforces awareness. The majority of products are 'launched' simply by getting them into distribution, with no further advertising, PR or sales promotional support.

Others

This heading suggests a list of also-rans, but this is in fact by no means invariably the case. Imaginative marketers will, doubtless, always be looking for new ways of attracting the right sort of attention to their brands, and novel ways may well make the communication especially effective.

Budweiser did itself a lot of favours with deft product placement in Tom Cruise's film *Top Gun*; the tyre company Goodyear gets a good deal of international publicity through their airship-mounted TV camera used to cover such events as motor-racing; and Richard Branson's personal exploits have done far more for the image of Virgin than any advertising could be expected to achieve. Similarly, designing ads that the media take up is a way of getting a lot of free publicity. This happened to a great extent with the UK's Greenpeace/Lynx anti-fur campaign; and in the commercial sphere with Carling Black Label lager. The possibilities certainly aren't endless but they are constantly arising, and those that spot and use them first not unreasonably garner the novelty dividend.

MAKING THE CHOICE

The above should have given you some sense of the diversity of communication tools at your disposal these days, and as a consequence the relative complexity of making a choice appropriate both to the communication objectives set for the brand, and of course the budget. In practice it also has to be said that beside these considerations, your decisions are likely to be much influenced by the status quo:

- existing lines of thinking inherited from predecessors working on the brand;
- existing arrangements or contracts between the company and its suppliers;
- existing practices of the competition.

As such the reality of the job is often to choose the best possible tools to meet the communication objectives, very much within the constraints of the status quo. This is a pity because the most effective communication packages tend to be the most radical and novel. This is for the very good reason that communication generally, and advertising particularly, is about getting people to sit up and take notice, and the radical and novel is a good way of getting them to do that. It is risky because it is untried, but that which is novel also has intrinsic virtues.

This means that although advertising remains the primary means of communication for most major brands, it's not the only way to do the job and neither is it necessarily the best one. For example, Marks and Spencer is a very strong brand that has used advertising minimally to build its franchise. Much the same could be said for Anita Roddick's Bodyshop – and, to a lesser extent, Richard Branson's Virgin. Moreover, as advertising in particular fields – tobacco, alcohol – becomes more and more restricted marketers will *have* to turn to other ways of protecting their brand's equity.

In practice advertising best justifies itself when:

- the brand is substantial or potentially so;
- there's a need to create or change public awareness rapidly;
- the sector normally uses advertising;
- the target audience is large;
- the spend available is substantial.

In the hypothetical world of the beer brand, what decisions should have been made? The problem there was that sales were being affected by the brand being seen as out of date, despite the fact that as a product the beer actually performed reasonably well. The communication objectives isolated were to improve the brand's image by repositioning it as a 'classic', and supporting this with the facts about cold filtration. So, the communication strategy might be as follows.

1 The spearhead of the communication programme will be *TV advertising*. This is because advertising is a crucial component of the communication mix in this mass-market arena, providing the most cost-effective way of rapidly changing consumer perceptions about the brand. The television will focus on representing this old brand as a 'classic'.

2 The TV advertising will be supported by a heavyweight *press campaign*. Good though television is at putting across feelings and images, it is less satisfactory at communicating thought and, in particular, detail. To explain adequately why the cold filtration process leads to a better quality beer, long-copy of press ads will be used.

3 A *sponsorship* will run in parallel, duplicating and supporting the idea expressed on television that the brand is a classic. And, rather than merely attaching the brand's name to an existing event, something new will be created especially for the brand.

4 The *brand livery* will be revised to take account of these activities, the communication audit having identified the fact the brand's faded imagery was exacerbated rather than challenged by its packaging.

You've now isolated what you expect the various tools to do to meet your overall communication objectives. In so doing you've completed the communication – and effectively brand – planning process and so may begin to feel that at least you know where you are, where you're trying to get to, and – broadly – how you're going to get there. You may also have decided that advertising *is* going to play a part in the communication. And it is at this point in the process that you may feel the need for an advertising agency.

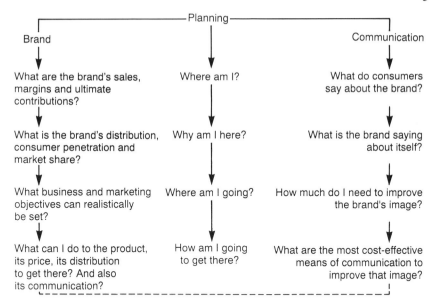

Figure 1.3 Brand and communication planning

CHECKLIST

1 Communication planning starts with understanding the brand's identity in the eyes of the consumer as much as it does with the more quantifiable issues like brand volume and share. This is part and parcel of the brand audit.

2 Having got under the brand's skin, looking at the various ways in which the brand expresses itself by means of a total communications audit provides clues as to why the brand is where it is.

3 Assuming that price, distribution and the product itself are not going to be major players in achieving the brand's marketing objectives, the next job is to set communication objectives.

4 As the various forms of brand expression – advertising, sponsorship etc. have quite different qualities, the chosen tool has to be carefully selected for the given communication task. This is the process of developing a communication strategy.

5 The essence of total communication planning is that the tools should be integrated. Each part of the package must complement or duplicate rather than contradict other activity.

6 Advertising is especially worth using as part of the communication mix if the spend available is fairly large, the brand has considerable potential, its target is large, and the need exists to create awareness or change imagery rapidly.

2 SOPHIE'S CHOICE
So you want to hire an advertising agency?

'Is Orr crazy?'

'He sure is,' Doc Daneeka said.

'Can you ground him?'

'I sure can. But first he has to ask me. That's part of the rule.'

'Then why doesn't he ask you to?'

'Because he's crazy,' Doc Daneeka said. 'He has to be crazy to keep flying combat missions after all the close calls he's had. Sure, I can ground Orr, but first he has to ask me to.'

'That's all he has to do to be grounded?'

'That's all. Let him ask me.'

'And then you can ground him?' Yossarian asked.

'No. Then I can't ground him.'

'You mean there's a catch?'

'Sure there's a catch,' Doc Daneeka replied, 'Catch-22. Anyone who wants to get out of combat duty isn't really crazy.'

JOSEPH HELLER
Catch-22

*Agencies not the only source of advertising · a short history lesson ·
agency structure · the full service agency and its cost · what agencies are really
selling · the advertising idea · alternative sources of ideas · supposed
weaknesses · when to use them · assessing your needs · making the choice*

Given that you've established that you do need to advertise, the next job is to hire an advertising agency – if you haven't already got one. Advertising and agencies go together like love and marriage and the horse and carriage, and an agency is naturally the first stop in seeking ads. Agencies generally select media more efficiently and buy it more cheaply than you can yourself; they think up and physically produce the ads as a matter of course; their creative work is supposedly of a high standard; and retaining an agency naturally marks you out as a serious advertiser and a professional marketer.

This though, is all beginning to change. Advertisers have begun to realise that agencies are very expensive sources of ads, that there are places –

little side-streets and alleys – where they can be obtained altogether more cheaply, and that a number of substantial companies advertise without using agencies and seem to advertise quite well. As a consequence more advertisers than ever before are reviewing traditional agency arrangements and putting full-service agencies on the spot. The question used to be: Which agency should we use? The questions now are: Should we use one at all? And if so, which services should we take? As advertisers strive to maximise the cost-efficiency of their advertising, these questions are entirely fair. Agencies, advertisers have decided, no longer have a God-given right to exist or to submit extra-large invoices at will. They may even have to answer the $64,000 question 'What do I get for my money?' Times have changed.

PERSONAL SERVICES

Once upon a time agencies were small, diffident, almost self-effacing businesses which made money by selling advertising space on behalf of newspapers. They were brokers, hawking vacant space to anyone prepared to buy it, paid on commission; they employed a couple of people and maybe a Dickensian office-boy; they had small, shady little offices in the less fashionable parts of town; they paid themselves a modest wage, and dressed and ate and drank accordingly. Anywhere they had to go they walked. Those familiar with the advertising business at the end of the twentieth century will appreciate that these times must have been either far away or long ago, and probably both.

Something that we might just recognise as advertising appeared shortly after the development of printing in the fifteenth century, rose with the coming of primitive newspapers in the seventeenth, and was sufficiently established by the eighteenth for Dr Johnson, apparently without irony, to declare, 'The trade of advertising is now so near perfection that it is not easy to propose any improvement.' After Johnson's death the burgeoning industrial and commercial society of the mid-nineteenth century fuelled an explosion of reading material, and space-selling became a more competitive activity. The agents consequently began to offer additional services to ensure that they took their commission, chief among which was a service offered one not to the paper but to the advertiser: agents began not simply to sell space, but to devise advertisements on behalf of the advertiser to fill it. For many this remained a subsidiary activity, but in due course the balance swung away from the straightforward business of brokerage towards the slightly more complex task of producing a combination of words and later pictures that people would notice, remember and, perhaps, act upon. The twentieth century had come. As with so much else, this arrived in America before it did elsewhere. It was here in the 1920s that agencies first became businesses of any size, and in America that organisations capable of planning, creating and putting proper advertising campaigns on the streets first came into being.

In addition to selling the space, dreaming up something to fill it and actually producing the ad, such organisations in due course came to provide two other services. Clearly, once a business is doing two things rather than just one, it's wise to have someone liaising between the two processes, and indeed between the service and the people buying it. This generated the account man, later to be joined in this garden of Eden by the woman. Then, following the media revolutions brought about first by radio and then television, advertising strategists or account planners emerged cautiously from agency research departments and tried to represent the views of the people whom the advertising was actually addressing, the 'consumer'.

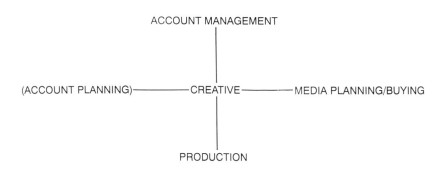

Figure 2.1 How agencies are structured

The consequence of all this was that twenty-five years ago something recognisable as the agency we now know had materialised. This comprised the basic disciplines of media-buying, creativity, account management and production, along with some sort of ancillary strategic or research function. Broadly, this is the form taken today by the top twenty or thirty agencies in most of the industrialised countries. They decide – with their clients – what the advertising needs to do and be, devise work more or less along those lines, buy the time and space in which it appears, and co-ordinate the whole process. They are the full-service agencies.

THE PRICE OF LOVE

Interesting or otherwise as all this all may be, the development and internal arrangement of the larger agencies is not in itself an issue here. The question is rather one of price and, ultimately, the value offered by these operations. Not very surprisingly the provision of all these services costs agencies in salary terms alone quite a lot, leaving aside the attractive offices in expensive central locations that have to be found to house all the people concerned. These are things for which the advertiser in the end pays, and pays quite a lot. This is not the place to discuss methods of agency remuneration, but whatever scheme is used, agencies these days worldwide probably extract by way of payment roughly 12 per cent of their total media expenditure on behalf of a client. So, if you're a typical advertiser using one of the larger agencies, you're probably paying the agency annually something in the order of $750,000. When the going was good, many advertisers took this as a cost of doing business. The view taken now by some is that this is an intrinsically large sum, if it can be regarded as discretionary then it is frequently the largest discretionary item annually expended; and not only is it the largest, it is also the least accountable, measurable and susceptible to evaluation. It is clearly something that at best needs to be very closely examined, and at worst – from the agency perspective – cut down to size.

And there's certainly little doubt that casting an eye over the agency service-versus-cost equation superficially produces some surprising results. In the final analysis agencies are like any other business in so far as they have something to sell. What they purport to, and to some extent do, sell is a full advertising service. The essence of what they sell today though isn't usually that full service. It is, as it has been for some time, not the media-buying but the creative service. Advertising agencies devise ideas and ideas are now their primary product. Of course, account people are there to sell the idea, planners to explain it, and media to place it, but the keystone is the idea. The argument, then, is a simple one. On the face of it the advertiser pays $750,000, annually, for the more or less assiduous attentions of a full-service agency. In practice it pays $750,000, annually, for an idea. And good ideas last longer than a year. A campaign based on a single theme or thought might last three or four years, very occasionally eight or ten. To an extent, of course, this is simplistic. Ideas have to be developed, themes varied, tactics devised, marketing directors lunched. Ultimately, though, it is close enough to the truth to pose the question: If what you're really getting from the agency is ideas, couldn't you buy them cheaper elsewhere?

NOTHING IS MORE DANGEROUS THAN AN IDEA

The answer to this question is patently 'yes'. There are two established groups within the advertising milieu, yet outside agencies themselves, which specialise in generating advertising ideas, and their costs are very considerably lower. First a number of companies – particularly newspapers and fashion retailers – retain *in-house advertising units*. These take various forms, but they focus on a creative resource responsible for the company's advertising, and often quite a lot else besides by way of point-of-sale material, window displays and the like. Media buying is normally farmed out. Secondly, the recession has bred all sorts of *creative consultancies*. As the phrase suggests, these too concentrate on the business of creating ideas but, like full-service agencies, they work for a variety of advertisers – sometimes agencies too – rather than being located within one. Other services like account planning and media-buying are bought in as occasion demands. Both these groups produce advertising ideas and – largely because of their lower overheads – they do so a good deal more cheaply than agencies. The only question is about the quality of these ideas.

This of course matters. It's an exaggeration to say that products stand or fall by the brands that are established to give them wider meaning, and that brands stand or fall by their advertising, arguably the brand's most powerful expression. But certainly some brands seem to have been made by their advertising, and others from time to time to have perished. The consequence of this is that advertising matters and that, in particular, the quality of the advertising idea matters. Advertisers need good advertising ideas rather than simply ideas, because advertising ideas can make and break brands. Less melodramatically, there's little doubt that some ads are better – a good deal better – than others, and the advertiser putting good money on the table will naturally want the better ones. The conventional view then is that you're not very likely to get good ideas out of anything other than an agency.

Consultancies, it is said, generally lack the strategic specialisation of full-service agencies, so they are not very good at producing the *right sort of ad*, however quickly they may produce *an* ad. They are also too much hand-to-mouth businesses to attract the best creative talent, tending to be formed when their personnel are thrown out of agency jobs rather than because they have spotted a gap in the market that genuinely needs to be filled. Moreover, the business arrangements between the advertiser and consultancy aren't particularly conducive to creating the best possible work. From the consultants' point of view the best way of running the business is to complete the project as quickly as possible, sell it and move on to the next.

This seems to argue against a long-term commitment to getting the work right – as opposed to getting it out – to preclude much feedback on the success or otherwise of the material (and hence its subsequent improvement) and diminish the gestation period that can be necessary to produce good work.

In-house units are held to have different problems, although again the arrangement – and in particular the salaries – supposedly militate against attracting the best talent. The chief problem with a company doing the job itself though, is often thought to lie in the proximity of the people buying the advertising to those producing it. People working in agencies can stand back from products and brands and – working as they do on a number of different campaigns – enjoy a degree of objectivity on their merits. Company cultures being what they are, this is a less easy process for those working for advertisers themselves. To an extent it may be a psychological necessity if you work for a company to believe that the services or products it produces are good. This means that the in-house unit is less good at seeing the brand through the eyes of the consumer – to whom, after all, most brands are worth scarcely a moment's thought. Secondly, agencies can reasonably – or, at least, quite reasonably – regard themselves as experts in communication and will therefore resist pressures to accede to your demands as advertiser as to what should or shouldn't appear in the advertising. With limited budgets it is entirely understandable that advertisers should wish – as they often do – to pack a quart into the pint pot of a single-page ad. Whether they are best advised to do so is another matter. In-house units are supposedly less able to resist this sort of pressure than independent agencies.

The extent to which this is all true now rather than in the past is a matter for some debate. It's a debate because there are, of course, no clear answers to the question. Some of the problems faced by these operations certainly do exist and doubtless affect the quality of the advertising; equally it might be very persuasively argued that agencies have their problems too, from inter-departmental rivalry and gross egotism, to power politics and so on. There again, recession has forced some very good ad people on to the market, and many enjoy working outside the constraints of an agency and appear to produce very good work.

The best evidence for either case naturally lies in the work itself. For a book that argues for a rather more considered and experimental approach to advertising, care has to be taken here. Good ads aren't necessarily pretty ads and a flock of creative award winners from consultancies wouldn't clinch the case – even if they bothered to enter. Good ads are those that do what they supposed to do against a set target. However, agencies used to be able to say with a fair degree of confidence that it was only kosher agency wares that were fêted in the press for their impact and were apparently highly successful. There's little doubt that in quite a few countries this has now changed, and that work publicly regarded as 'good' is emerging from places other than accredited agencies. How does this happen?

Now advertising agencies being equitable, reasonable, tolerant and democratically run organisations naturally regard all advertisers as equal. However, they will very occasionally recognise some as being more equal than others, and some may even be regarded as 'good clients'. A good client, from the agency's point of view, buys the work and pays the bill without question. These paragons are rare and in any case they aren't really good clients. Good clients are actually those familiar with the ways and wiles of advertising agencies, familiar with the sometimes tortuous process with which work is produced, and people who accordingly are capable of getting the best out of them. And they by no means invariably pay their bills on time. These people *do* exist, they understand advertising, they can judge advertising, and they are capable of extracting decent ads from a creative consultancy, an in-house unit or – come to that – friends around the industry. Whether they wish to, or have the time to do so is another matter, but the option is certainly there. It is the existence of these people, perhaps in growing numbers or perhaps more interested in advertising than they were, who are challenging the dominance of the agency.

Even if you aren't such a being, there are still circumstances in which the full-service advertising agency isn't the solution. Typically those are when either time or money is of the essence, or the job is small and/or relatively straightforward. Big agencies generally work slowly and charge a great deal for so doing. This is not really because 'creativity' is an intrinsically time-consuming process, nor because it is intrinsically expensive. Rather it is because agencies are relatively large organisations with a number of jobs on hand at any given moment and with considerable overheads in addition to the payment of the creative staff. This means that if you need something done quickly or cheaply the full-service agency isn't the place to go. That's also the case if the job is a small one. Agencies familiar with working on multi-million pound television campaigns are perfectly capable of producing twenty doubles for your spouse's favourite charity, but they are unlikely to be very interested in so doing. This is very much an occasion on which you should go elsewhere.

This all means that the alternatives to the full-service route do have a case and perhaps increasingly have a case. The real question is then how big a case it is. It certainly exists if you're a highly experienced advertising buyer and it exists if you've got a small job you want done cheaply or quickly. That said, it is less likely to exist in other circumstances and those other

	Creativity	Cost	Speed	Size of job	Client expertise
Full-service agency	✓✓✓	X X X	✓	Large only	Valuable
Specialist service	✓	X	✓✓✓	Small only	Crucial

Figure 2.2   Agencies versus the rest

circumstances are perhaps generally those that prevail among larger advertisers. Pretty clearly these are when the company isn't a highly experienced advertising buyer, and the job's a big and important one. And it is on these occasions that the large agencies still remain your best bet. They have a good record in producing advertising for such clients in such circumstances. It's not that you can't do it yourself. It's simply that as someone in that position you are *more likely* to get good advertising out of an established, sizeable agency.

A LA CARTE AND TABLE D'HÔTE

It follows that the real answer to the question of agencies versus the rest lies in looking very carefully at your advertising requirements. Ultimately, the 'full-service' agency proposition posits the extreme case of an advertiser with relatively limited communication and advertising expertise who needs to buy some people in to do the majority of the advertising job. At the opposite end of the spectrum lies the company with considerable such experience which has the time and resources to adopt the à la carte approach by taking the agency services it needs and not bothering with the rest. Your job as an advertiser then lies in accurately and honestly assessing where on the spectrum your company lies, and exactly what its advertising needs are.

Of the various aspects of agency service, the assumption is that creativity

goes without saying, and that with that really has to come account management. Some agencies insist on this liaison service. And in any case it is
probably true that most advertisers are best advised to use it, on the grounds
that they will get better work in a shorter space of time if they use professional advertising managers to run what is normally a trying process.
Whether you then need research/planning and media-buying is then more
debatable. With certain brands in certain product sectors there's little doubt
as to what the advertising should be saying and how it should be saying it, so
there's little need for someone to do the account planning job. Equally,
when launching a new brand or conducting some fairly radical repositioning,
a planner is a good investment. The merits or otherwise of using media
independents, as opposed to the agency's own service, are discussed in
Chapter 8. It is enough to say here that you are likely to get better media
planning and buying from people who thoroughly understand your brand,
and what you are trying to do with it, and that these people are more likely to
be found in the place that is producing the advertising. The phrase, however,
is 'more likely', not 'will always'. It is up to the agency to demonstrate that
the first phrase applies. For the majority, the evidence will probably still
favour the agency, and then the issue becomes which one to choose.

CASE–HISTORY 2
Benetton

The Benetton campaign is so far the most controversial of the 1990s.
　Founded in 1965 by the Italian Luciano Benetton, Benetton manufactures
and retails casual clothes. By 1990 it had a network of 6500 independent
shops, a turnover of £2 billion and a decidedly global vision – Benetton views
Europe as the 'domestic' market and the rest of the world as its future.
　Patently a successful company, it is tempting to associate its growth at
least partly with its devotion to publicity. This takes two main forms: the
long-running sponsorship of a Formula 1 motor-racing team with the global
TV coverage that achieves; and the advertising. The latter is the brainchild
of Luciano Benetton himself, and the photographer and film director
Oliviero Toscani. Their campaign run since 1984. Actually campaign is
probably a misnomer in the sense that its taste for controversy has much
developed over the years, as also has its theme. Originally the work took the
form of what were in effect corporate statements of Benetton's multi-
cultural vision. For example, one of the first ads – All the colours of the
world – featured groups of people of different races and colours enjoying
themselves together. The strap-line was United Colours of Benetton. Their

more recent work – a new-born child, a nun kissing a priest, a mercenary clasping a human thigh-bone, a bird covered in oil – could not be so described. The billed objective of this work is 'to take the role of protagonist in the confrontation of ideas on important topics'. This is startling as an advertising approach because of the extent to which it is divorced from the more obvious objective of an ad campaign for Benetton – to help establish it as a good place to buy pullovers.

In Benetton's own view, the controversy the campaign has aroused is 'proof that the company has achieved its advertising objective'. Slightly more rigorously, UK research run by *Marketing* magazine's Adwatch survey indicates the very high levels of advertising awareness that you'd expect of the work. Equally predictably, there was evidence that the ads – particularly the baby – weren't greatly liked. It is a question as to whether or not this matters; and one of opinion too on what the campaign has done for the brand's image. Benetton apparently conduct no research on the campaign. Either way, this is striking work from an 'in-house' unit – if Benetton and Toscani can be so described. It is interesting too that Benetton's media-buying is now all carried out in-house.

CHECKLIST

1 **The recession has meant that advertisers should be considering very carefully whether they should retain an advertising agency or employ more ad hoc arrangements.**

2 **As agencies are essentially sources of ideas which are very expensively priced, it should be possible to get the same thing elsewhere more cheaply.**

3 **Although advertisers are more likely to get better advertising ideas more frequently from an agency, instances of work like the Benetton campaign suggest that when the advertiser knows what it is doing, the agency now isn't the only option. Moreover, when time and money are at a premium, big, full-service agencies are to be avoided.**

4 **Choosing the full-service route or going it – to a lesser or greater extent – alone, depends on the level of advertising expertise of the advertiser, and the nature of the advertising the company needs.**

3 THE MARRIAGE OF HEAVEN AND HELL
Getting into bed with an agency

Once, when Osbert Sitwell was speaking of his parents, I asked if there had ever been a moment when they got on well together. 'Oh no,' he said. 'Not for a moment. I don't think so.'

ANTHONY POWELL
Messengers of Day

Choosing the right agency · criteria for the long-list · creativity and creativity · the sources of information · compiling the short-list · importance of lunch · getting the best out of pitches · big brands and small projects · buying presentations not presenters · choosing a client · terms of business · payment · payment by results

Assuming you've decided on the agency route, the next job obviously enough is to hire one. Although apparently an opportunity to meet some reasonably interesting people and pick up some free advice and a number of gourmet lunches, choosing an agency is actually at best an irritating job, exacerbated by the fact that, especially in a recession, advertising agencies are unbounded in their enthusiasm to choose clients. Anyone in charge of a significant advertising budget is constantly pestered by agency new business people seeking meetings, and, if any whisper of a review reaches the press, they are absolutely inundated. When the tourist board of one of the English Channel Islands let slip it was reviewing its $600,000 advertising account, it supposedly received 124 approaches overnight. With this level of interest from agencies in finding clients, the problem is altogether less how to find an agency than how to find the right one. And finding the right one matters. It is true that virtually any of the thirty largest agencies in any country is likely to provide reasonably professional advertising. But it by no means follows that all of them will do a good job on a particular brand for a particular company run by particular people at a particular time. The production of advertising is a peculiarly collective effort in which it is crucial to achieve the best possible mix of agency experience, talent, and convergence of corporate culture, together with a personal chemistry between the people on each side of the agency/client equation. So choosing the right agency follows the process of total communication planning as the second step in your getting the best advertising possible.

EVERYTHING YOU ALWAYS WANTED TO KNOW ABOUT ADVERTISING   AGENCIES

However pressing agency new business people may be – and it is their job to be pressing – there is clearly little point in going in to see an operation for that reason alone. Rather, it is wiser to compile a long-list of agencies based on everything discoverable about them without actually visiting the places. The principle in sifting through this information is not so much whether or not the agency is intrinsically any good, but more whether – like Guinness – it would be good for you. Bearing this in mind, the main criteria are as follows.

Creativity

Creativity is a much-abused term. It should mean the effectiveness of the advertising the agency produces and, as such, should be by far the most important way of judging it. In fact, the word is used more loosely. It usually means simply that the agency produces work regarded by the industry as good. Far from meaning that it 'works' or is highly cost-effective, this suggests merely that the advertising is aesthetically attractive or entertaining. This is all very pleasant in its way, but the fact is that the link between attractive and effective work is debatable. Work which pleases the particular and peculiar people working in the ad industry may or may not be liked by – or ultimately influence – its real audience. The chief criteria in selecting an agency should accordingly be less creativity than, as far as possible, the proven impact of the advertising on its target, ultimately leading to some form of sales effect. Creativity generally and creative awards particularly should be of minimal interest to a potential client.

This is, of course, all fine and dandy in theory, but may be less so in practice. Advertising evaluation remains a primitive art and can't simply be reviewed like a company's report and accounts. Moreover, the major source of opinion of the advertising's effectiveness is the agency itself. Many agency presentations to prospective clients take the line that all their advertising is tremendously effective. Under pressure they may grudgingly concede that some campaigns could be more effective than others. One way round this is to ask their existing clients. Agencies don't normally volunteer such references. There's really no reason why they shouldn't.

Size

Size matters in an agency less because it is a measure of financial success or indicative of the quality of its advertising – neither is necessarily the case – more because there should be a reasonable fit between the size of an advertiser's advertising budget and the size of the agency. There are certain large agencies with outstanding reputations constantly cited in industry research as being advertisers' first choice should they wish to review their existing advertising arrangements. This isn't terribly sensible because small to medium-sized accounts are, in financial terms, insignificant to large agencies and, as a rule, they will be inadequately serviced by junior staff. Equally, advertisers should have very good reasons for dominating an agency. If the account represents more than a quarter of agency billing, the agency and its staff are generally too dependent on the account to permit the degree of autonomy and straight-talking crucial to producing decent advertising. Agencies in these circumstances tend to give their clients more what they want than what they need – something that to be fair, many clients are entirely happy with. The ideal is when the billing represents an important contribution to the agency but not a vital one.

Growth

Advertising is a notoriously volatile business in which the fortunes of agencies can change quickly. Losing business doesn't necessarily mean that an agency isn't any good, and winning business doesn't mean it's brilliant; but these factors are related, and anyone who puts an account into a sinking ship will want to know in some detail why the leaks appeared in the first place and how securely they have been plugged. Moreover, advertising over the last twenty years has been a growth business and will, presumably, be so again. This means that agencies that aren't growing in billings terms are actually losing market share. Prospective clients will doubtless wish to know why.

Market understanding

Does the agency know the market? This seems to be an important question, and the general assumption is that a thorough knowledge of a given market is crucial to producing effective advertising. However, if the agency is familiar with the market it's probably working for a competitor and convention debars it from being hired. (Whether this is a good convention is debatable. 'Chinese walls', which act to isolate the stockbroking part of a company from the conflicting business of market-making, work quite effectively in certain financial centres.) In any case, although some markets are certainly quite complex and it is accordingly pleasant for advertisers to have a reasonably knowledgeable agency, the relationship between encyclopedic market knowledge and good advertising rarely seems causal. The London agencies handling the major car accounts have done so for some time and presumably know the markets inside out. With perhaps one exception, few in the advertising business would make very large claims about the excellence of the sector's advertising. Moreover, unless as an advertiser you need an agency that works as an extension of an overstretched marketing department – and few agency people, whatever they may say, really know much about marketing – agencies are capable of learning as much as they need to know about markets for advertising purposes quite quickly. At the stage of preparing a long-list market knowledge is thus desirable more than vital.

Reputation

Given the difficulties of objectively evaluating the merits of advertising produced on behalf of other advertisers, subjective qualities such as reputation inevitably play a part in the selection of an agency. This is reasonable in so far as reputations aren't created out of thin air. However, a general reputation may be independent of specific ability on a specific brand, or indeed whole advertising sectors. There are clear cases of agencies with strong 'creative' reputations which have consistently failed to work successfully with advertisers, say in the retail area, requiring not so much pretty ads, rather more a more workmanlike approach. Similarly, some agencies are far better at one medium than another. Many agencies that are good at television cannot seem to grasp the essentials of press, and vice versa. Finally, it is often the case in a business so dependent on individuals that those who created an agency's reputation have now moved on to more lucrative jobs elsewhere. Image normally substantially lags behind reality and you may find it illuminating to ask the agency how many of the ads on the reel were produced by those still working there.

All this means that reputations shouldn't be taken quite at face value. Bad ads can come out of very good agencies.

Resources

Resources too are less a general point than something which should be related to an advertiser's own requirements. Those with no ambitions to advertise abroad and no interest in direct marketing will rightly feel the existence of such provisions to be beside the point. Conversely, if you've got a relatively complex advertising problem, and you believe in the importance of the integration of the media and creative functions into the whole advertising process, you will want an agency with thoroughly established planning and media departments.

Financial status

This is sadly more an issue now than hitherto. It goes without saying that in any business relationship the financial stability of the two parties is paramount. Leaving aside the evident unwisdom of booking into a hotel that's about to go broke, agencies with money problems will naturally concern themselves more with those than the servicing of their clients. As a consequence it is necessary to have quite a careful look at an agency's finances before proceeding very far with them. This examination should concern itself both with signs of failure and those of success. Although profiteering in advertising as a whole, as opposed to particular aspects of invoicing, is now fairly rare, it certainly hasn't been in the past. Advertisers will reasonably resent undue levels of profitability on their business.

Personnel

Marketing and advertising in many countries is a trade in which everyone knows everyone else. If you've established a good relationship with an ad-man in the sense of someone who understands your needs as an advertiser *and* can deliver against them – often very different things – that's a contact worth maintaining, and even following from agency to agency.

The appendix at the end of this chapter is an exhaustive agency checklist adapted from one prepared by Britain's Incorporated Society of British Advertisers.

There are various sources of this information. In most countries with established advertising industries there are *advertising agency guides* available for prospective clients. These are useful up to a point, but should be treated with a degree of caution. The majority tend to be compiled by agencies on their own rather than on the behalf of advertisers, and are therefore uncritical in their tone. They are in themselves advertisements. A guide compiled by advertisers on their agencies would be useful and might make entertaining if occasionally libellous reading. *The trade press* – marketing and advertising – is often a more impartial source of news and views on agencies. Even here though, it is worth remembering that most trade publications need to remain on the right side of the industries on which they report. This means that the general approach as well as specific treatment of particular topics, or agencies, is not invariably as impartial as the reader has the right to expect. In the UK there is a service called the Advertising Agency Register which provides an opportunity to see the *promotional videos* agencies periodically produce. The AAR staff are also well informed on the status of agencies, and on issues such as which are going through the periods of flux generic to the industry, and which are more stable. There are one or two comparable services in other countries. *Consultancies* are dating agencies designed to bring prospective partners in the agency/client liaison into happy conjunction. Theoretically justifiable on the grounds of the importance of appointing the right agency, it is less than apparent what they bring to the mix unless the advertising buyer is inexperienced or from overseas. Their proliferation is probably more a consequence of ad-men looking for jobs than meeting long-felt needs. Last, but by no means the least important as a source of information is *word of mouth*. There can be no stronger recommendation for an agency than the impartial assessment of other ad people, marketing people or, as already suggested, advertisers with which the agency is working.

These sources should enable you to put together a long-list, ideally of no more than six or seven agencies, in which your company is sufficiently interested to go and visit. Within that list it is sensible to have a certain amount of variety. Given that all meet the parameters suited to your bit of business as opposed to Mars's or Sony's, different sorts of agency are likely to treat your problem in different ways. For instance, it might be sensible to include the following.

- The hottest agency in town. Invariably there's always one that is the flavour of the month, normally in terms of winning new business.
- A couple of well-known top twenty agencies, likely to produce highly professional work.
- A more stolid and worthy operation, to produce 'safer' work.
- A new start-up. For obvious reasons these places often try harder, and tend to provide senior staff to work on small pieces of business.
- A left-field choice. There's usually an agency around with a reputation for providing surprising solutions to advertising problems. These are worth hearing and, sometimes, pursuing.

Alternatively, if you have a very clear view of the sort of advertising you want or need, you may choose the same number of agencies but draw them from a narrower spectrum of the market. If the man or woman who signs off your advertising has the imagination of a split pea, is is probably best to look only for the stolid and worthy, with perhaps one wild card thrown in.

Having compiled the long-list, make the agency MD's day by telling him you're coming in.

WHEAT AND CHAFF

The purpose of the next stage of the selection process is to make a short-list of agencies that you want to pitch for your business. It normally takes the form of adding to the impression of each agency that has already been made through the preliminary sifting by actually visiting the places. The overall purpose of this is for the agency to get a decent initial sense of the people with whom it would be working and the advertising problem they're expected to tackle; and, more importantly, for you to get some idea of the agency, its personalities, their calibre and, perhaps above all, the agency culture. By and large these meetings are indifferently handled by everyone involved. So, it is important to do the following.

1 Give the agency *decent notice* – three weeks – of your intention to come in. Some advertisers seem to imagine that agencies have nothing better to do than wait for the knock on the door. This is in some respects the truth, but it's rarely the whole truth. Once you are an established client you will resent the time spent by the agency on new business prospects, because it is often at the expense of your own.
2 Be specific as to who you want to meet and what you wish to cover. In normal circumstances that should start with the *standard agency credentials* presentation. This is the agency's opportunity to sell itself. If it can't do that it is not so unreasonable to suppose that it can't help you sell your products. A surprising number can't. You will also want to meet the *people who might work on your account* should the agency win the business. And you should ask them to prepare some brief thoughts on *your market and your advertising*.
3 It is worth while having *lunch* after the presentation with senior agency personnel to cover those subjects less suited to formal talks, and let all parties get to know each other better than the formality of the meeting permits. Naturally the agency will pay.

It is inevitable at this stage of the process that the business of selection will become more subjective, depending less on facts and figures, and more on whether you like the overall feel and impression of the agency and its personnel. Nevertheless, it is worth preparing a checklist of points that you should look for, and on which you and your colleagues can compare notes afterwards. Here are the chief questions you should ask yourselves.

- Who appeared at the meeting, what level of seniority were they and how competent did they appear?
- What were the points they tried to communicate about the agency and its work? Were they in an absolute sense good selling-points, and did they have any relevance to your own communication problem ?
- Was any serious attempt made to relate the creative work to an individual advertising problem, and show results? If so, how plausibly was it done?
- Did the agency manage to say anything novel, imaginative or true about your market, or existing advertising?
- Did they appear to be people you could work with, preferably displaying a similar way of looking at marketing and advertising problems ?
- Was the whole meeting efficiently managed?

What you should look for at this stage is energy, enthusiasm, a *degree* of experience in the product sector, concrete evidence of strategic, media and creative skills, some elements of personal chemistry, and some evidence of similarity between your own company's and the agency's culture. You shouldn't expect an encyclopaedic market knowledge or a pat solution to a problem which your existing agency spent some time failing to solve.

These visits enable you to compile a short-list. In the market research business in Britain it is contrary to the established code of practice to ask for more than three research agencies to pitch for any piece of business. Really, there's no reason why a similar practice shouldn't obtain with ad agencies. It is unreasonable to expect agencies to expend the sums of money they often do on pitching without an adequate statistical chance of success. And if your own choice in the past has been good, there's no reason why one of the three shouldn't come up with a good solution to your problem.

If the incumbent agency is asked to pitch, a short-list of four is acceptable. Whether it should be asked is another matter. Generally, if the relationship has broken down to the extent that a pitch has been called, the sense in asking it to try again is limited. It's also limited statistically, in that only a small minority of incumbents retain business in a repitch. Some companies appear to be reasonably satisfied with their agency but use a pitch as a way of keeping them up to the mark. There must be better ways of achieving this objective and if the pitch isn't a serious one it is a scandalous waste of time and money for the other agencies.

THE PITCH

The normal way of proceeding from this short-list to the appointment of an agency is the pitch. Usually this involves giving each agency a brief and asking them to come up with provisional strategies, media and creative recommendations against it. Although this is not a foolproof process, it is certainly the best way of selecting an agency because it forces them to do some spade-work on your market, consumers and brand, requires them to come up with a plausible and superficially workable advertising solution, and ensures that they do so within a relatively short space of time. For an advertiser these things are obviously highly desirable. Moreover, they are also things which, left to their own devices, agencies either simply don't do, or will do at their leisure. Thus, appointing a new agency on the basis of whether their faces fit, or giving an existing agency a new brand on the strength of its work on another within the company's portfolio, is a mistake. The pitch is the thing.

That said, it is a good deal more questionable whether it's sensible to ask the agencies to prepare work on a major brand, speculatively, in the time normally available for pitches. This genuinely requires a lot of work which, generally, isn't done or isn't done properly – and the work presented is rarely that which is actually run. Moreover, the agency is only being paid at best nominally for the pitch work. Agencies resent working as free consultancies, and who can blame them? The upshot is that it is often sensible to ask agencies to pitch on a project, a small brand or a subsidiary problem. This enables you to get the feel of how agencies work and what they are likely to produce, without asking too much of them in the time available.

Having decided to run a pitch and what the substance of that pitch should be, you've now got to run it. There are good and bad ways of running a pitch – good and bad more precisely in so far as there are circumstances which can be created that give the competing agencies the best possible chance of producing the best possible work, and those which often prevail that don't. Here's how to get the best out of the short-list.

1 Give the agencies a reasonable amount of time for the pitch, but not too much. There is no reason why it should take a competent agency more than six weeks to get its head round what should be a fairly small project. If it takes or needs more, it is either incompetent or cannot manage its time. If you give agencies more time, most will get bored and won't start on the project till the last moment. Generally, three-quarters of the work is, in any case, done during the last week before the pitch, sometimes in the last thirty-six hours.

2 Prepare a thorough written advertising brief, approved by all those who will be making a decision on the candidates. Such papers are of a very variable standard. They should cover:

(a) an overview of the market, key competitors, and the brand's strengths and weaknesses;

(b) summary project business and marketing objectives;

(c) a definition of the role of advertising within the marketing mix;

(d) an assessment of the strengths and weakness of any existing advertising;

(e) the criteria on which the new work will be judged.

3 Give the agency a thorough, formal face-to-face briefing. There are invariably issues and nuances that cannot be covered in writing. Even if it's a small project, agencies should be given the chance to talk these through at as senior level as possible.

4 Give the agencies an opportunity for less formal briefings once they've actually started work. To describe what you want in words is a very different thing to seeing it encapsulated in an ad. One of the best ways of speeding agencies up the learning curve is therefore for them to show you work in progress before the pitch. This enables you to say: less like this, more like that. Agencies which are precious at this stage over the production of creative work and the assimilation of your comments are not going to be easy to work with in future.

5 Give the agencies a clear idea of exactly what you expect them to cover at the pitch. All will obviously give their views on the problem, but one or two these days are still coy about producing creative work. Many advertisers will feel that this is absurd.

6 Outline your ideas about remuneration. This will normally be a case of your own company's standard practice, but you should be prepared to listen to the agency's own proposals in due course.

The qualities by which pitches should be judged are precisely those by which advertising should generally be assessed, and form the substance of some of the remainder of this book. Suffice it to say here that the chief questions to ask yourself are the following.

• Has the agency understood the essence of the brand's market position and marketing problem?
• Has it accurately identified and defined what the advertising should do?
• Is the proposed advertising strategy sufficiently in tune with the realities of the brand, is it relevant to the consumer, and is it distinctive?
• Does the creativity correspond with the strategy, and do you think it will work?

- How imaginative are the media proposals, and how impressive are the proposed costs?
- How does the agency propose measuring the campaign's impact?

The problem in answering these very reasonable questions is that pitches tend to be very theatrical occasions on which it is all too easy to be swept away in a flood of rhetoric and eloquence from very far from retiring personalities, and fail to distinguish this from the real thinking behind the advertising and the real merits of the work. People buy the presenter, not the presentation – presumably because they are more familiar with making assessments about people than they are about more abstract notions of advertising strategy and more subjective notions of creative work. Yet ultimately consumers see the work alone, without the sophisticated strategy or the creative person in the Armani suit, pony-tail, cowboy boots and peanut-butter tan. Hence, important though it is that advertisers feel they can work with agency teams, the ads themselves should be the main element by which the pitch should be judged. It's for this reason that the best way of making a decision is to take away the work of each of the agencies, and in a separate meeting debate the work and the work alone. On the basis of that judgement, you can hire an agency.

HOW TO CHOOSE A CLIENT

Or you can if the agency will let you. Of course, if things have got this far it is a very rare agency that turns a client down at the altar, but it is perhaps worth remembering that agencies choose – or should choose – clients as much as advertisers choose agencies. As has been suggested, the advertiser's job is not that of finding and hiring a good agency, it is about choosing the right one for the company and the advertising task. Similarly, decent agencies – except perhaps in a recession – don't chase advertisers of any shape, size or disposition willy-nilly. Most have a fairly clear view of the sort of clients they wish to add to their client list, and a more or less – normally less – rigorous process of approaching and occasionally winning that business. That view will depend on a number of issues that it is worth being aware of.

The first is the *nature of the client's business*. Some sectors are either intrinsically attractive to agencies or are seen as complementing existing pieces of business. FMCG (fast-moving consumer goods) is big business in most countries and there are few agencies that don't aspire to take a share of the cake. At the same time, the sort of advertising done on FMCG – goods like soap-powder, toothpaste and coffee – is normally fairly unimaginative. 'Creative' agencies often aspire to FMCG clients because they think it will help other large, conservative advertisers take them more seriously. The other side of that coin is advertising for charities. Agencies frequently see this as a good opportunity to do exciting, noticeable, creative work, charities being seen as subjects for advertising of intrinsically greater emotional force than for fish-fingers or baked beans. The view is that such accounts rejuvenate jaded creative departments and attract industry attention. For this reason some agencies are prepared to run such accounts at a loss.

There are also certain sorts of business that agencies should, and sometimes do, avoid. Those with high creative reputations often shy away from retail accounts on the not unreasonable basis that the price-lists forming the basis of much retail advertising will diminish their standing. It is also widely believed that such accounts are work-intensive and difficult to run profitably. Similarly, there is often a question-mark over media clients, particularly newspapers. Of a creative bent themselves, these outfits tend to have little respect for advertising agency creativity and less for agency timescales. People turning round national newspapers in twenty-four hours can be unimpressed with agencies incapable of producing one radio script in three weeks.

Next is the likely *profitability* of the account. Unlike the nature of the business, this isn't easy to predict until the client is actually in the fold. Still, it's normally possible to make some sort of prediction and, for obvious reasons, it is a necessary one to make. There *are* reasons why agencies will carry nominally unprofitable pieces of business, but in the end – normally the beginning too – agencies are in it for the money. One of those reasons may be the expectation of a *client's growth* or, strictly speaking, growth in advertising spend. Generally the work done on a client's business substantially precedes the time at which the agency is paid – at some point after the work is aired. Often with new products and launches this situation is exacerbated. Agencies are occasionally prepared to invest resources in such projects in the expectation of substantial billings if the product is a success. Both these points are related to the issue of the client's *financial stability*. Because of the way in which the business works – agents are agents rather than principals – agencies generally aren't heavily exposed to their clients' financial uncertainties. Nevertheless, agencies are small businesses that need their bills paying promptly.

There's also the issue of *compatibility* to consider. The relationship between client and agency is very far from an easy one, and it is not particularly unreasonable to ask the question: 'Can we work with these people?' Money being concerned, the view agencies almost invariably take is 'yes', but whether that's in the best long-term interests of the collective effort of the advertising, the agency or agency personnel is sometimes more debatable. The bottom line on client/agency relationships is just that: the client is a client and most agencies to a lesser or greater extent at least superficially take the stance that the customer is always right. Yet, companies have radically different cultures when it comes to doing business and there needs to be a reasonable fit in this area if the relationship is to be a fruitful one. At its simplest this can boil down to an inclination or otherwise to take risks, but there are also quite divergent ways of looking at marketing and advertising issues, which in some companies are firmly entrenched. Advertisers and agencies at the opposite poles do well to keep apart.

Finally, there is a significant minority of advertisers and a significant minority of *individuals who abuse their position* and in so doing destroy any possibility of creating effective, complementary working relationships. This is rarely apparent before the deal is signed, but the subsequent consequences are disagreeable. Agencies and individual clients can be, and sometimes are, sacked.

Still, before this rather drastic and happily unusual ending to the relationship comes to pass, it has in the first place to begin. This means agreeing terms. These vary from country to country but are normally and quite usefully set out by local associations of advertisers and agencies. Terms of business usually cover such things as copyright, the confidentiality of client material and, more entertainingly, terms of notice. More importantly, they specify the services the agency is supposed to provide, and at what cost.

MONEY, MONEY, MONEY

There are two basic ways in which agencies are compensated for their services. The time-honoured method is that of commission on the advertising space taken, now normally in the order of 12 per cent. This pays the agency on a pro-rata basis, depending on the cost of the campaign. The bigger the spend on the advertising, the larger the agency's gross income. The oddity of this is that it is not, of course, the *agency's* expenditure that rises with the cost of the campaign, it is the advertiser's; and often the agency work-load on a medium-sized TV account is significantly less than on a busy little mixed media retail account half its financial size. For this reason – among others – the system is gradually being replaced by fees. To some extent this is an improvement because at least it means that the agency is paid – roughly speaking – in proportion to the amount of time it spends on its client's business. This will be bad news for the small retailer and good news for the television client, but overall it appears to be a more equitable system. Moreover, it gives advertisers the option to pay for the agency services they want and not for those they don't. The growth of media independents means that not all clients want a media service. Some, too, refuse to pay for any strategic input.

Conversely, a moment's thought suggests that there's also something odd about the fee principle. Advertisers are paying not for what they get, but what it costs agencies – plus a little more – to provide that service. The third alternative is therefore to pay the agency not in accordance with its costs, but with the value of its service to you the advertiser. Advertising is an investment on which a return is expected and the agency is paid in proportion to the size of the return. Needless to say, there is as a beginning a certain pleasing natural justice to such a scheme; more importantly it provides a fairly urgent motive for agencies to contrive results which the alternatives significantly lack. The snag, of course, is the permanent difficulty of assessing the impact of a major campaign, let alone more modest advertising efforts. Nevertheless, the media-buying activities of agencies are increasingly assessed in such a way, and there is a growing inclination on the part of advertisers to put other aspects of the account on that basis. In practice this usually means providing the agency with a basic income and adding a performance-related bonus. Where such schemes are already in operation the bonus is generally dependent on the subjective analysis of the client brand team on the merits – essentially – of the agency service. As it becomes gradually more possible to evaluate advertising activity (rather than agency service), the impact of the advertising should be the criterion on which agency fees are based: in short, payment by results.

The other issue is how large this total sum – however arranged – should be. In circumstances in which advertisers and their agencies are both having a hard time, this is inevitably a sensitive issue. Advertisers with accounts in their gift are themselves seriously short of money; agencies are often desperate for business. This leads to a situation in which some advertisers are making proposals that ultimately add up to no more than a commission of 5 or 6 per cent. And some agencies seem to be accepting deals along these lines. This is a sad reflection of the current state of the industry, for it is only a very short-term solution and a poor basis for what is supposed to be a mutually beneficial business relationship. A better one seems – again – to give the agency a basic income plus a considerable incentive to perform.

Having dealt with all these little matters – deciding that you need to advertise, deciding that you need an agency, deciding on the right one – the first phase in the advertising cycle is complete.

Britain's most popular advertising

Making the jam go further.
Free publicity for Carling Black Label

O.T.S.

Mills & Allen. Maiden Outdoor.

An opportunity to see creative targetting, courtesy of Mills & Allen

"Make the logo bigger."

The marketing director's dying words

Product poster

Corporate brand TV ad
'I want to be a slug'

Product TV ad
'You're a bit young to be a pensioner'
'*Prudential* pensioner'

Product leaflet

Integrated communication: Before (1989)

Product poster

Corporate brand TV ad
'I want to be a tree'

Product TV ad
'We want to be together'

Product leaflet

Integrated communication: After (1991)

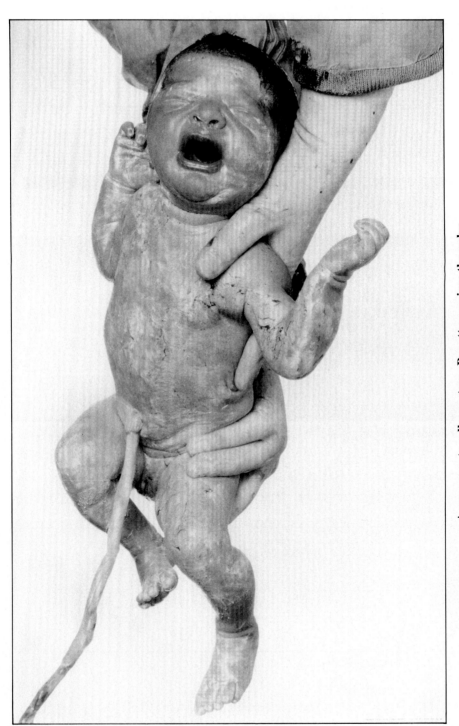

A new way to sell sweaters. Benetton waives the rules

Love conquers all

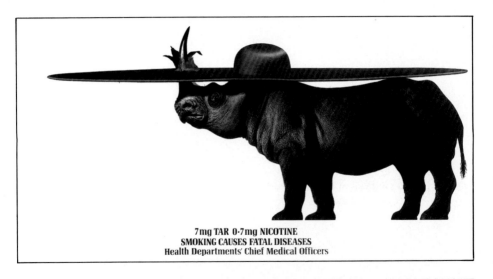

7mg TAR 0·7mg NICOTINE
SMOKING CAUSES FATAL DISEASES
Health Departments' Chief Medical Officers

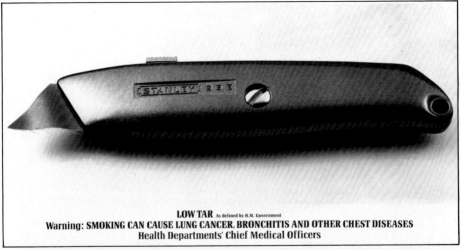

LOW TAR As defined by H.M. Government
Warning: SMOKING CAN CAUSE LUNG CANCER, BRONCHITIS AND OTHER CHEST DISEASES
Health Departments' Chief Medical Officers

LOW TAR As defined by H.M. Government DANGER: Government Health WARNING: **CIGARETTES CAN SERIOUSLY DAMAGE YOUR HEALTH**

Silk Cut cigarettes. The advertising *is* the branding

CHECKLIST

1 Make sure you choose an agency rather than an agency choosing you. In a recession the tendency for the latter to occur is heightened.

2 Don't look for a good agency. Look for one that would be good for you. These two things can be very different.

3 Prepare a long-list of no more than six agencies on rational criteria like size, advertising effectiveness and reputation.

4 Prepare a short-list of no more than three or four on more subjective criteria, notably on the compatibility of individuals between your own and the agency's team, and the level of cultural convergence between the two companies.

5 Insist that all the agencies pitch for your business, and in so doing prepare creative work. It is sensible to get them to work on a small pilot project rather than a major brand.

6 Judge the pitches on the presentation and the work rather than the presenters themselves.

7 Motivate the agency by ensuring that at least a proportion of its fees will depend on how well the advertising works.

APPENDIX: ADVERTISING AGENCY CHECKLIST

1 **Quality of top management**
   Is the agency's top management professionally competent in advertising and marketing?
   Does it have drive?
   Is it organisationally well set up?
   Is it stable, or likely to change?
   Is it over-committed? Would they have time for our business?
   Are they reliable?
   Do they inspire confidence?

2 **Staffing**
   Is the agency adequately staffed?
   Is the quality of lower management good?
   Are they prepared to buy in talent, if needed, for our business?

Are account personnel experienced in marketing?
Is the staff organised on well-defined lines?
How easy is contact across the agency departments?

3 Creative ability

Does the agency convince in its ability to produce 'creative' advertising that sells the products?
Is it well staffed creatively?
Are the creative groups (copyscript writers, layout, visualisation, typography, creative research) well linked?
Is the creative talent dominated by any one personality?
Does the agency specialise in any creative style?
Does it keep its creative talent?

4 Research

Is the agency able to understand and interpret research figures?
Does the agency employ creative research as standard practice?
Does the agency charge for this service?
How are the results of research assessed, and by whom?

5 Campaign planning

Does the agency have clear plans as to how they work with their clients?
Do they have any system of quality control once the campaigns are under way?
Can they show evidence of how they have built successful campaigns?

6 General

Does the general appearance of the agency, its offices, layout, furnishings and the conditions of work all inspire confidence?

7 International

Is there evidence to show that the effectiveness of the agency benefits from an international association?

8 Recognition

Is the agency recognised by local advertising and media associations?

9 Client/agency agreement

Are the terms and conditions of the contract fully acceptable?

10 Services

What services are located in-house and which are bought in?
How are these co-ordinated and how charged?
Can the agency handle exhibitions, literature, press relations, audio-

visual presentations, internal communications schemes etc.?
Do you in fact need all these services?

11 Financial

What is agency turnover today and historically?
What is the size of the largest and smallest account, average account size and how does this compare with your projected spend?
Is the agency financially stable?
How is the agency to be remunerated, commission, service fees, price per job, time rates or combination of charges?
What are the agency's preferred invoicing procedures and general trading conditions?
How are production costs charged?

12 Agency classification

Is the agency predominant in any one area-consumer, industrial, direct response etc.?
Is the majority of work in any one sphere – press, TV, radio etc.?
Do they have experience in your markets?
Do they have or have they held accounts competitive to yours?

Source: Incorporated Society of British Advertisers.

PART TWO

What the Awards also demonstrate, of course, is that spending advertising money does not automatically create a return on investment: it only does this if the agency and the client between them have got it right. And sometimes that the difference between getting it right and getting it wrong is not just a matter of 5 or 10 per cent at the margins, but between a campaign which generates extra profit and a campaign which is a complete waste of every penny spent on it.

PAUL FELDWICK
Boase Massimi Pollitt/Doyle Dane Bernbach

4 LIKE A ROLLING STONE
Setting advertising objectives

Like a rolling stone, with no direction home.
BOB DYLAN

Objectives more likely to be achieved if set in the first place · distinguishing between business, marketing and advertising objectives · a definition of advertising · setting objectives · quantification · setting objectives against budgets · difficulties of · the empirical approach

The job so far is not going badly. You know more or less where the brand stands in the eyes of the consumer; a total communications audit has indicated how and in what ways the various bits and pieces of communication are contributing to the whole; some brand marketing objectives and strategies have been established; and it has been decided that advertising does have a part to play in the communication mix. Accordingly, you've hired an advertising agency.

This is when the hard work of extracting good advertising really begins. It starts with setting objectives for the advertising against which – at the end of the advertising cycle – it can be fairly objectively assessed. This perhaps should go without saying, but the fact is that agencies – and advertisers – are occasionally rather less precise about nailing down exactly what the advertising is supposed to do than might be expected. On the grounds that you are more likely to reach a given destination if you've decided in the first instance what that will be, this is something worth addressing.

OBJECTIVES AND STRATEGIES, STRATEGIES AND OBJECTIVES

The context of setting ad objectives has already been touched upon, but it's worth reiterating here for the purposes of clarity. The beginning is the business objective for the brand, normally expressed in terms of revenue, margin and profit. Marketing objectives are then set by way of such things as consumer penetration, distribution and market share. These are, in effect, strategies by which the business objectives can be achieved. Marketing strategies derived from these involve such things as fiddling around with the product, ensuring that its price remains at the very least competitive, and seeking greater distribution. If there is limited room for manoeuvre in these areas, the burden of marketing activity falls on the communication package. The overall objective of such communication work is – generally – to improve what people think or feel about a product or a brand without actually changing the reality of that product. The choice of communication tools – sponsorship, direct marketing, advertising etc. – then depends on the precise nature of the job to be done. In this way, advertising objectives depend on communication objectives, communication objectives depend on marketing objectives and strategies, and marketing objectives depend on business objectives. Or they should do, anyway.

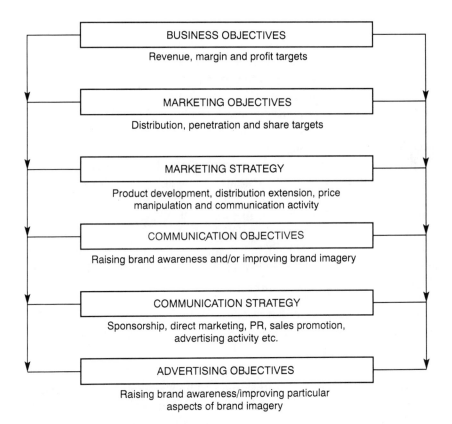

Figure 4.1 Developing advertising objectives

This may all seem rather pedantic but it is worth thinking about because these strategies and objectives, while interrelated and interdependent, are not exactly the same thing; and because there is a tendency to assume that they are. The commonest of set advertising objectives – defined by agencies as well as advertisers – is to 'increase sales'; the next to 'launch' a new brand. Advertising alone is unlikely to achieve either of these things. It can participate in the task of increasing sales by playing a part with – say, a sales promotion and a distribution drive – in increasing brand saliency. It rarely 'increases sales' because unless it is a direct response ad it does not seek directly to do this. Similarly, advertising can't 'launch' a brand. If the brand comprises a decent product at a reasonable price which has achieved or is expected to achieve an adequate level of distribution, it may help the launch by creating awareness of the brand that otherwise would probably exist only at a low level. Advertising, therefore, plays a part in the launch by doing something that it can do: create brand awareness. This is not something that it alone can do, but rather – among a large target audience – it is something that it can probably do more cost-effectively than other means.

It follows that the cardinal step in setting advertising objectives is to set objectives that advertising *by itself* can accomplish. If this doesn't happen, advertising is in effect being asked to do something that it can't do, and you and the agency are going to get into a terrible tangle when it comes to assessing whether the advertising has worked.

WHAT DO YOU WANT THE GIRL TO DO?

This begs two quite important questions: what exactly *is* advertising and what precisely *can* it do? As suggested, it cannot do a number of things that it is often asked to do by way of launching brands, relaunching them, increasing sales, achieving higher levels of consumer penetration and growing market share. Rather, it can contribute to what are actually marketing, not advertising objectives by achieving what is best defined very simply as *communicating information*.

These two words are worth dwelling on for a moment. *Communicate* is important because it means convey or put across, rather than simply state or express. Most companies are entirely capable of telling their consumers what they want them to believe about their brand. They pay advertising agencies lots of money because agencies bring statements to life, capture the public's imagination and therefore *communicate* ideas that are then (often) remembered, and (sometimes) used. So much for communication. The other point is that the *information* communicated isn't any old information, but is restricted to information about products and services – occasionally causes and charities, sometimes points of view. Advertising objectives that concern themselves with anything other than communicating information aren't – strictly speaking – advertising objectives.

If this is advertising, then what can it do? This is best answered by asking what *sort* of information does, or can, advertising convey? Or rather, what sort of information about goods and services does it convey? This too – at least at this stage – should be answered as simply as possible. Advertising generally conveys two basic sorts of information:

1 that intended simply to make potential purchasers *aware* of a new product or service in the first instance, or to increase awareness among the target – making more people aware;
2 that designed to make them *think or feel* differently about an existing product or service.

Again, the same principle applies. An advertising objective that isn't related either to brand awareness *or* what people think or feel about a brand isn't, strictly, an advertising objective. And, as a consequence, it shouldn't be set as a task for advertising.

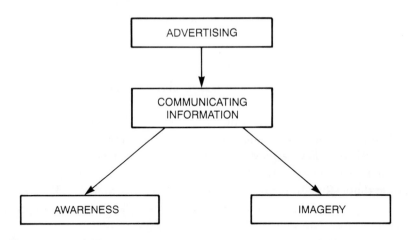

Figure 4.2 What is advertising?

The issue then becomes the extent to which it's necessary to create, increase or merely sustain brand awareness; and which sentiments or thoughts about the brand you need to change, which the advertising should focus on. What you need to do on any given brand will obviously depend on its status – as revealed in the brand audit. At its simplest, if you're launching a brand, the primary job of the advertising is likely – at least in the first instance – to be to create awareness; if you've got a mature brand, it will be to change imagery in some way. These really *are* advertising objectives, in the sense of things that advertising by itself can reasonably be expected to do. Of course, this isn't to say that the advertising shouldn't ultimately concern itself with behavioural objectives. Growing brand awareness is all very pleasing in its way, but it is likely to be part and parcel of a drive to increase the numbers of people who actually use the brand. Similarly, 'image' advertising may well seek to dispel the view, say, that cornflakes should only be eaten at breakfast – with the intention of increasing 'usage occasions' and hence the rate of a brand's sale. Such things are best seen as secondary advertising objectives because they usually depend for their achievement on other marketing variables.

So much for the objectives themselves. The other thing that has to be considered here is the issue of their quantification. For instance, given advertising's two basic qualities, it might be reasonable to set advertising the task of (a) raising brand awareness by X per cent, and (b) increasing agreement on an image dimension that the advertising was focusing on by Y per cent. This sort of requirement is in fact set in certain countries – notably the US. The argument against it is that there are things other than advertising affecting brand awareness and imagery, and therefore an advertising effect – where the advertising has been responsible for the change – is difficult to derive. The fact is that it *is* difficult to derive and it's rarely possible for the assessment to be entirely objective. Still, some sort of figure usually *can* be derived – especially in terms of awareness; and the increasing need for advertising to be accountable argues in favour of setting such objectives. It is difficult to demonstrate to advertisers that their campaign has been effective unless measurable objectives are set for it in the first place. Setting specific goals also, like the prospect of hanging, concentrates agency minds wonderfully.

It might be added that this isn't a particularly new idea. R. H. Coller in 1961 developed the idea of DAGMAR – (Defining Advertising Goals for Measured Advertising Results). This was a process which aimed to plan advertising by selecting and quantifying advertising objectives. Like many good ideas it seems to have been largely forgotten.

MONEY

The missing link in this discussion is the advertising budget. If you have to set your advertising objectives in the context of business, marketing and communication objectives and if they have to be advertising, not marketing objectives too, they also have to be compatible with the budget set. This is another of those points that seems obvious, but is in reality by no means common practice. As has been remarked, as a marketer you're often informed of the company's business objectives for the brand, allocated a budget on the basis of what is available, and told to go away and derive marketing and advertising objectives accordingly. The problem here, clearly enough, is that the business objectives dictate the marketing objectives, the marketing objectives dictate the advertising objectives, and these objectives may be – and often are – too ambitious for the budget available.

This is a fact of life in the 1990s, as it has been for many years. However, this in itself is no reason not to try to improve matters. Of course, setting advertising budgets is a thoroughly imprecise business, partly because of the general, central difficulty of predicting what a certain form of advertising with a particular spend behind it will achieve. Given that it *is* difficult, the tendency is to give up trying to predict what such activities *will* achieve and, more reprehensibly, not trouble unduly with the slightly easier task, which has a bearing on future spends, of determining what such advertising previously *did* achieve. This seems a shame because it militates against notions of accountability and value in advertising.

There are, in fact, all sorts of ways of deciding how much in theory should be spent on the ads, one diligent writer describing seventeen. In practice, though, in so far as principles are applied to setting budgets beyond allocating what's left in the till after pay-day, the advertising-to-sales (A/S) ratio is normally used. This is the arrangement whereby a set proportion of gross revenue is creamed off and given to the marketing department for advertising purposes. This ratio or proportion varies quite dramatically from market to market, and even to some extent logically. Where product differentiation is low, the power of brands as a consequence considerable in encouraging consumers to discriminate between similar products, A/S ratios are high, with up to 10 per cent of revenue ploughed back into advertising on certain cosmetic items. Conversely, where the unit cost is high and there are some genuine differences between products, the decision to purchase is often rather more rational and considered. Here, branding and advertising may play a somewhat smaller part, and the retailer a greater one in influencing consumer brand choice. A/S ratios in such markets – say in cars – are normally far lower, sometimes by a factor of ten. Many advertisers take the A/S ratio as their bench-mark, the extent to which the average is exceeded or undershot naturally depending on the marketing director's influence on the board.

Logical though this might all seem, in practice it isn't a very good way of setting a budget. As a moment's thought suggests, it is a recipe for stasis in so far as the central, often unstated, idea is to remain at par with other advertisers in the same sector. Stasis is the objective for some, but by no means all brands, and when launching, relaunching, repositioning or seeking a burst of growth, a spend two or three times the typical A/S ratio may be required. Equally, as a principle it ignores the idea of the creative multiplier, discussed later in the book. This simply means that some ads – some campaigns – are a good deal more effective than others, by a multiple that some suggest may occasionally rise to something like fifteen. From this it follows that to spend proportionally the same as your competitors is somehow to imply that the creativity or impact of your advertising is comparable. This is relatively rarely the case and in certain instances the disparities are genuinely dramatic.

A better idea is in fact the first step towards a more empirical approach to advertising. This argues that what you should do in theory is ignore competitive spend and the sixteen other ways of computing what to budget, and spend what you need to spend against your targets, using your advertising. Then, the only way in practice of determining what the figure might be is to try it and see. This means in practice sticking to the A/S sector benchmark for the campaign as a whole, but varying it considerably in a couple of test areas. Obviously this is far easier said than done when large sums of money are at stake, but even on established brands with established campaigns it is surprising how little experimentation is undertaken in such matters. Varying the weight of advertising by area is relatively easily done in countries with regionally discrete media, and its results are *relatively* simple to check. Bearing in mind the sums involved, examining the effect of increasing or diminishing spend to determine the optimum level is well worth while. And the interesting thing is that a significant number of brands appear to spend more than they really have to.

A/S ratios should therefore only be your starting-point in discussions, even better in trials, concerning how much of your company's hard-earned cash you really do have to spend on the ads.

CHECKLIST

1 Advertisers and agencies are sometimes less careful about setting objectives for advertising than might be imagined.

2 These objectives have to be carefully related to the business and marketing objectives from which they stem. At the same time, they are distinct from

these objectives. Marketing and advertising objectives are often confused.

3 Advertising objectives should generally concern themselves with raising (sometimes maintaining) brand awareness, and influencing specific and specified aspects of brand imagery. There is a good argument in favour of their quantification.

4 Advertising objectives aren't always related with sufficient thought or care to advertising budgets. As the impact of advertising is dependent on all sorts of variables, its useful to experiment with advertising weights to try to find optimal levels to achieve set objectives.

5 DEVICES AND DESIRES
Creating advertising strategies

'I wonder who it was defined man as a rational animal. It was the most premature definition ever given. Man is many things, but he is not rational.'

OSCAR WILDE
The Picture of Dorian Gray

Advertising strategies · do they matter? · different sorts of advertising · tailoring message to target · targeting · deficiencies of existing systems · alternatives · what to look for in a strategy · product versus brand values · the perils of research · strategies for the 1990s · tone of voice.

You've decided what you want your advertising to do. Now the issue is one of strategy, how to do it, or at least, how the agency is going to do it.

Actually, strategy – like so much other marketing vocabulary – is vaguely used, and as a term often embraces the advertising objectives themselves and, more legitimately, the issue of the people whom the advertising is addressing, for strategy depends to an extent on the definition and nature of the advertising target. It also usefully covers the issue of the advertising's tone of voice.

These matters seem important and perhaps they are. Advertising strategists will certainly tell you they are because it's their job to do so and without a strategy they wouldn't *have* a job. Art directors and copy-writers probably won't agree. They will argue that it is sufficient merely to advertise, and that all discussion of the precise message of the advertising, its exact targeting and tone of voice is beside the point. The medium – the very fact that the brand is advertised – is the message. This brand matters: it is successful enough to advertise; it follows that it is worth trying, or buying again. It's difficult not to have some sympathy with this argument, while at the same time feeling that a strategy appropriate to the advertising objectives, the brand and its consumers is more likely to be effective than one which isn't. So, how to develop a strategy.

FOUR TYPES OF ADVERTISING

When talking about broad advertising objectives, the suggestion was that there were two basic sorts of advertising: that intended to create *awareness* of a product in the first place, sometimes to increase or sustain it; and that intended to make consumers *think or feel differently* about a product or brand they already know about. This is fine as far as it goes. Now it needs to be developed. The first sort – awareness advertising – can remain. But the idea of advertising encouraging people to feel differently about brands needs to be divided up into three separate, although related areas. These are, first, advertising that *reinforces* existing beliefs; then that which *challenges* them; and, finally, advertising that *entertains*. The point about this sort of categorisation is less that advertising invariably does these things, nor that other categorisations are not possible; rather that it is a straightforward and practical way of thinking about advertising strategies.

1 So advertising can *create awareness*. Marketing people – most of them anyway – have long appreciated the falsity of Emerson's suggestion that he who builds a better mousetrap will find the world beating a path to his door. People generally have better things to do than buy mousetraps and they certainly won't seek them out unless they've heard of them in the first place. Although there is sometimes reason to give the public the impression that they've discovered things for themselves, more often than not they need to be made aware of new lines, new products, new brands. So the first job that advertising can do is to create that initial awareness. It's worth adding that this is a particularly useful function in so far as there's much value in novelty. Most people have a limited repertoire of brands and products that they use in any given product field – cars, watches, pullovers, hairpieces etc. – and they tend to buy as much by force of habit as by active and positive choice. Many welcome the opportunity to try something new.

Advertising can also usefully and quite cost-effectively *increase* awareness, (although they may need it for other reasons). Given that time exists. This last point is sometimes forgotten. Brands that lots of people buy and use regularly probably don't need advertising to sustain awareness, (although but they may need it for other reasons). Given that time passes and lots of other companies are urging consumers to try their brands, awareness of less frequently used brands will naturally decay. Advertising can help halt this process, and it is entirely legitimate that it is used largely to maintain the status quo.

2 It can *challenge*. Given that successful brands have quite long life-cycles

and that consumer tastes gradually change, it's common for advertising to be used less to affect public awareness of a brand than to change attitudes towards it. Thus, if the majority of brands in any market have identifiable strengths and weaknesses, the job of advertising is to challenge people who have negative beliefs about a brand.

3 It can *reinforce*. If a brand is in good shape it may be necessary for advertising to do no more than reinforce existing positive beliefs about it. As has been suggested, the fact that people forget about things unless they're reminded and that there are always competitive brands clamouring for attention, means that even if the brand communication objectives are merely to maintain the status quo, it's still often necessary to advertise. If people's beliefs are broadly positive, then the job is to support and underline, rather than challenge them.

4 It can *entertain*. This is the fourth basic category of advertising and perhaps superficially the least logical. The argument is that in product arenas in which there is relatively little functional or rational in consumer motivation on which advertising can hang its hat, a more oblique approach is called for. Instead of focusing on negligible differences between one product and the next, it tries to establish an empathy between the brand and its consumers. If this is established, the consumers' goodwill has been obtained, and that goodwill often seems to be translated into purchasing behaviour. By entertaining people – not directly selling them the product – their goodwill is obtained.

These ideas are clearly not mutually exclusive. Advertising can enhance awareness by challenging, and may well entertain and create goodwill while

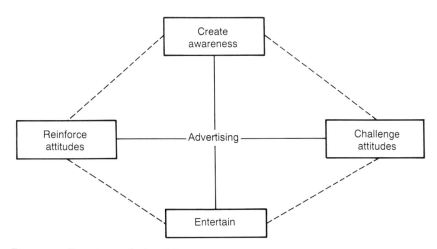

Figure 5.1 Four types of advertising

reinforcing existing attitudes. However, the basic categorisation is useful because it focuses the minds of advertisers and advertising agencies on the idea of isolating the chief job they think the advertising should do. This will, of course, depend on the state of the brand and the profit expectations from it in the manner outlined earlier. If the brand's in fundamentally good shape the job is essentially to reinforce existing beliefs. If in less satisfactory form, the job is to challenge . . .

REAL PEOPLE

Given that a decision has been made as to which quadrant your advertising fits into, the next job would appear to be to sort out how to do it. This is essentially the issue of the advertising's message. However, in fact the message is dependent not only on the objectives of the advertising but also against whom it is targeted. Given that most brands of any size are bought by relatively large numbers of people, it is inevitable that there exists a spectrum of attitudes towards and behaviour associated with the brand. In behavioural terms there will be everyone from the utterly committed loyalist who buys a jar of Nescafé every week, to those who buy it on the occasion of the mother-in-law's annual visit. And attitudes will, broadly, match: regular purchasers tend to be well disposed towards products; occasional purchasers less so. Two things follow. From the advertising point of view it's sensible to prioritise a target within this overall spectrum, in line with the findings of the brand audit. Is the brand's problem that it is, for instance, failing to recruit new consumers, or that it's failing to hang on to existing ones? This matters because the message appropriate to the loyalist isn't necessarily the right one for the occasional purchaser. Using the model already established, if you need to target those already using the brand quite often, the job is likely to be to reinforce existing attitudes. Conversely, occasional buyers are more likely to need to have their views challenged. It follows that the advertising strategy generally, and the precise message of the advertising particularly, are dependent upon the target. It also means that targeting is in itself something that needs to be pursued with some care if the best is to be obtained from advertising.

In practice, advertisers and their agencies are sometimes reluctant to make these decisions and ask advertising to do a number of jobs against the whole marketing target. This is the brief that reads that the role of the advertising is to increase repertoire, frequency and penetration against an 'all men' target. The danger of such an approach is sufficiently obvious. This is that it tries to do all things to all people and ends up doing none.

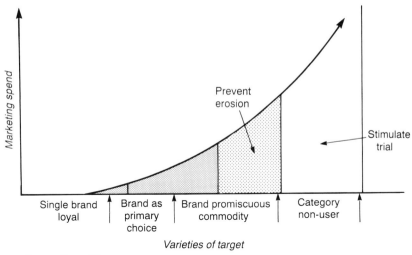

Source: Payne/Stracey

Figure 5.2 Segmenting the target

Conversely, advertising targeted as tightly as the medium permits can be highly beneficial. In seeking a message and a manner of expression most likely to influence a particular part of the brand's target to feel or do something specific, it is clearly likely to achieve the object – of, say, challenging. As a spin-off, this may well work, although in a different way, against a secondary target. These people might be existing users of the brand who need only to be reassured of its merits by the simple fact of seeing it advertised.

You can, of course, object to all this by saying that advertising can't really be targeted. Certainly it is true that advertising is a broadcast as opposed to a narrowcast medium, meaning that by its very nature it addresses large numbers of people, and that it is difficult to use it discretely to address the smaller groups who might be established as the most important target for the advertising. How can you isolate a target among the millions who watch *Cheers, Neighbours, Coronation Street* or *LA Law* each week? Yet while targeting a broadcast medium is difficult, it's far from impossible. The commercial television companies which live or die by advertising are daily more active at delivering to advertisers relatively definable and discrete groups. Similarly, particular sections within newspapers, like motoring or women's pages, provide opportunities for reasonable levels of targeting. Moreover, it is not simply the media that can be targeted. So too can the message and its manner of expression. The poster companies – always sensitive to accusations of wastage in what at first glance seems to be a medium that's quite untargetable – have in England recently run a campaign directed against the marketing and advertising industries. In using such marketing terms as Cover and OTS this was a good piece of *creative* targeting.

Another point worth remembering is that the target is less of the pool, as marketers are sometimes wont to imagine, than a stream. Unless as a brand owner you're happy with the idea of sales being in slow decline, it is always necessary to recruit into a brand because at the other end of the spectrum there will always be people abandoning it: sometimes because they are promiscuous, sometimes because they no longer need the product – for instance nappies – sometimes simply because they die. This means that it is important to consider not only who *is buying* the brand and who you would *like to buy* the brand at any given moment, but who is going to be buying it in five years' time. This is particularly important in the US and most of western Europe, because the demographic changes that are now occurring in these markets are the most dramatic of the century. In broad terms the west has an ageing population, and more interestingly and specifically these changes can have quite extreme implications for marketing products in certain sectors. These sorts of change clearly challenge marketers. They should, for instance, get them to question the sense of, say, targeting a brand at a diminishing demographic sector. Would repositioning it to attract more mature consumers be wise? Should the brand age with its consumers?

Finally, the people who *buy* brands aren't necessarily the same as those who choose them. Children, for instance, don't – or shouldn't – have the money to buy, but their influence on many decision-making processes is

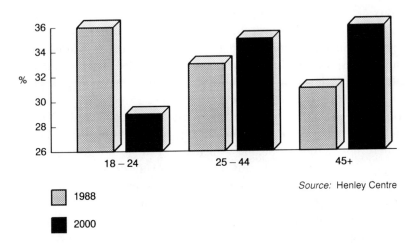

Source: Henley Centre

Figure 5.3 Why demographics matter: age profiles of pub visiting 1988–2000

crucial. This is something that the brand audit should have established, but it's worth reminding yourself of this at the targeting stage.

So, targeting advertising campaigns can and should be done. The final issue is how it is best done. This normally involves a segmentation of the market – all those who do, or might, buy the brand – into bits. The conventional method of so doing is by socio-demographics, pigeon-holing people in terms of:

- how old they are;
- which sex they are;
- which social class they belong to;
- where they live.

The advantages of this system are that it is very widely accepted and understood, it's employed by the biggest and most important of the syndicated marketing, market research and media usage surveys, and it is, in certain respects, quite actionable. This means that if you identify your existing brand users as mainly 25–45 ABC1 men, you can actually buy this group on television, and you can recruit them on a brand monitor to see if they're getting your advertising message. The only snag is that it doesn't really work. For a scheme that is so widely accepted this is a pity. The essence of any system of good segmentation is that it discriminates. This means that instead of just cutting up a market or a large, heterogeneous group of people into parts, it cuts them into parts that differ in ways that are significant and actionable. For instance, it is largely true that luxury cars are bought by socio-economic group AB more than C1; and in this sense the socio-economic grouping discriminates. However, it doesn't discriminate very usefully because it doesn't distinguish between people who buy Mercedes on the one hand and Jaguars on the other. Both these marques are bought predominantly by ABs. The segmentation fails to discriminate between different brands operating in the same sector. As such, from the point of view of developing targeting, the system is not specially helpful.

This means that it's almost always necessary to build on socio-demographics by finding alternative methods of segmentation. Broadly these fall into two groups:

- more sophisticated methods which apply to most markets
- segmentations tailor-made for particular markets

Life-stage

You can apply this idea to a number of markets. It acknowledges the fact that age, sex and class are often less helpful ways of isolating a target market than an individual's stage of life. While two twenty-four year olds share the demographic quality of age in common, the one who is single and still living with his parents is likely to differ radically in terms of how he lives, and therefore what he buys, from someone of the same age living with his wife and young child in the house next door. At its simplest, the bachelor will spend his disposable cash on beer and the married man on nappies; the bachelor wouldn't be caught dead in the local supermarket, while the married man may have an account there; Friday night at the Dog and Duck for the one is on, for the other it is very much off. Here the segmentation is discriminating and discriminating usefully for the owners of brands whose appeal depends on life-stage. There's little point in targeting nappies at twenty-four year olds. There's every point in targeting young marrieds. The five life-stages usually identified are the *teens*, the period of *establishment in employment*, the business of *family formation*, the *empty-nesters* after the family has gone, and the *retired*. Others can be imagined or contrived.

Sheep and goats

This, too, has general application. The idea is that people can be usefully grouped according to their enthusiasm to adopt new ideas and more specifically to try new brands. It's based on the readily observable fact that some lead while others follow, and that people can be motivated by their wish to be seen as belonging to one group or another.

Tailor-made

These two methods – there are others – are quite widely used as approaches to all sorts of markets and are often useful. However, it's often the case that none of the ready-made systems of segmentation really distinguishes between buyers of your brand and those of competing brands, and that when it comes to targeting and prioritising targets, you're at a loss. None of the established systems seem to distinguish between those who buy Brand X and those who buy Brand Y. Yet something is likely to distinguish these people, otherwise they wouldn't be so locked into their own brands. Something in one brand's values must appeal to one group more than another. On this occasion *lifestyle* – as opposed to stage – may provide a clue. This means that if there is nothing in the more obvious pieces of segmentation like age, sex, income and class which distinguishes between buyers of your brand and the competitive brands, there may be something in the consumers' way of life that inclines them towards one brand rather than the next.

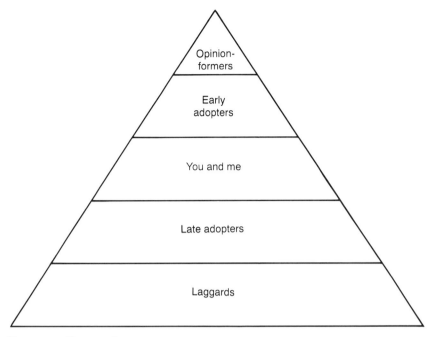

Figure 5.4 Sheep and goats

In Britain, a series of 'lifestyle statements' have been added to a national survey of purchasing habits called Target Group Index (TGI). The range is limited, but can be useful. The way to use it is to see if there are statements that you suspect might discriminate between your brand and its competitors, and check if that is in fact the case. This is easily done in so far as TGI correlates purchasing behaviour with lifestyle statements, and may well be able to produce a series of statements that collectively segment a product category and distinguish between users of one brand and the next. In the US there is a comparable system called VALS (Values and Lifestyles). Table 5.1 shows a series of statements selected to try to isolate the characteristics of users of a brand of premium exotic food.

Table 5.1 Lifestyle statements

	Desired Response
We usually have roast on Sundays	*Mildly disagree*
I normally read the recipes in magazines	*Strongly agree*
I like to try out new food products	*Strongly agree*
We usually have a snack meal in the evening	*Mildly disagree*

Continued overleaf

Table 5.1 continued

I really enjoy cooking	*Strongly agree*
My newspaper has very good articles on food	*Strongly agree*
My family rarely sit down to a meal together at home	*Mildly disagree*
I enjoy eating foreign food	*Strongly agree*
Ideally I prefer to take holidays off the beaten track	*Mildly agree*
I would never think of taking a package holiday	*Mildly agree*
When I go on holiday, I only want to eat, drink and lie in the sun	*Mildly disagree*

THE GOSPEL

These procedures will help you and your agency decide who needs to be the main target for the advertising and what broad form that should take: whether it needs to announce, challenge, reinforce or entertain. Having done so, you can now go on to the central issue of advertising strategy: what actually needs to be said. More exactly, you need to consider the following.

- If you need to announce something, of precisely what do you need to inform your target?
- If you need to challenge, what exactly is likely to encourage the re-evaluation of the brand you want to achieve?
- If you need to reinforce, which positive brand values are likely to be the most persuasive?
- If you need to to entertain or obtain the target's goodwill, how is this best achieved?

Clearly the answers to these questions will be, as ever, dependent both on the particular product sector and on the nature of the brand. Nevertheless, it is possible to lay down general guidelines which apply to all four basic forms of brand advertising:

1 As Chapter 1 suggested, the starting-point for brand strategy lies in the issue of *consumer motivation*. It is easy to think that people buy newspapers because they want to read the news, not least because they may tell you so in consumer research. But the fact is that they have heard the news already on television or radio, that they like reading, and that glancing through the paper is a pleasant and stimulating leisure activity. Effective

advertising will exploit such understanding. Similarly, health warnings on cigarette packets may positively appeal to the young. The forbidden and the dangerous to some have great allure.

2 Say something that is as far as possible *unique*. Advertising specifically and brand-building generally are about creating unique identities or meanings for brands. To claim that a brand has a property which it merely shares with other products in the sector doesn't greatly contribute to this. Consumers not unreasonably expect everything that competing brands offer, plus something else. And if that something else isn't more, it should at least be different. 'Product interrogation' usefully summarises the process of finding something to say about a brand, the idea being 'to interrogate the product until it confesses its strengths'. Leaving aside the fact that people generally buy brands rather than products, this is useful.

3 Conventional wisdom also dictates that *what is said should be true*. This is perhaps less helpful. While it is certainly undesirable – and indeed contrary to various codes of advertising practice, the Ten Commandments etc. – that advertising should propagate lies about a brand, it is less important that the claims should be true than that they should be *related to the defined advertising task*. The claim that is true is not necessarily the one that will 'challenge', and that which challenges is by no means invariably the one that will reinforce. Facts about brands have to be used selectively.

4 If this narrows the field, the need also to be *relevant to the chosen target* may do so further. A claim may be unique and it may fit in with what you are trying to do with a brand, without being particularly germane to the people you're talking to. For instance, claims about a brand's success – World's Favourite Airline, World's Best Music Stores – don't tend to appeal to 'early adopters' because, by definition, they prefer to lead rather than follow.

5 Say something that you're likely to be able *to go on saying*. There's not much point in spending a lot of money making a brand claim which is likely to be overtaken by such events as competitive entry. Of course it is sometimes possible to make a generic property, for example high cost, the brand's own, and in Britain Stella Artois lager has done this effectively with the stance 'Reassuringly expensive'. Generally, however, it is better to look for long-term properties in areas in which it is difficult for competitors to make counter-claims.

6 Be *single-minded* by saying one thing, not two or three. It is perfectly reasonable to say that people buy brands for various reasons, and it might logically follow that these various reasons should be incorporated in the advertising. Unfortunately, advertising doesn't work that way in so far as

it can't really effectively communicate more than one basic message. In a 30 second or 40 second TV commercial, a radio ad of a similar length, a press ad or a poster, you cannot hope to convey to someone, who is not very interested in what you're selling anyway, more than one idea. If you try, you are more likely to communicate nothing at all rather than the two or three things intended.

7 Say something that is *susceptible to dramatisation*. The cleverest strategy is not so clever if it is very difficult for the creative department to bring to life, and in this sense the process of developing a strategy is one which has to be carried out very much in consultation with the agency creatives.

This is quite a long wish-list, which could lead to a lot of agonising for you and your agency. In practice though, the most important thing to keep in focus is the *general motivation* of people buying brands. As has been remarked, perhaps the most striking thing about advertisers, and to a slightly lesser extent their agencies, is their disinclination to see things from the point of view of the people they're actually advertising to: the consumer. To advertisers and their agencies brands matter. Advertisers work on the same brand day in, day out, sometimes for years. Agency people are in the more fortunate position of normally having several brands in their portfolio, but even they are obliged to take each one moderately seriously. In both instances, salaries depend on looking after the brand. It is their job. In many respects few perspectives could be more different from the consumer's. The extent to which particular individuals interest themselves in shopping for branded goods naturally enough varies quite considerably. For few people though, could it be considered a job. Perhaps most people in the course of a normal day buy one item that at some time has been advertised. This doesn't take a great deal of time and neither, generally, a great deal of thought. People don't, as a rule, spend hours in supermarkets weighing up the pros and cons of individual brands of baked beans. They are in a hurry to get to the bank before it closes and fetch the kids from school.

Arguably, these two perspectives – on the one hand the advertiser and the agency, on the other the consumer – differ merely in degree. The former are very, very, very interested in the brand, and the latter have a passing interest in it, occasionally. In many product fields, though, it almost certainly goes beyond this to the extent that the differences are really those of kind. Ultimately it is simplistic to say that the brand owner views the brand rationally and the consumer emotionally, but this may at least be a useful piece of shorthand. It means that brand owners are inclined to think in terms of extra strength, extra flavour, extra features, extra pages. Their customers are often rather less sensitive to specifics of product delivery and tend to buy brands more on a self-referential basis: whether or not the brand is for 'people like me'. They may possibly rationalise the choice by reference to some aspect of the product, but the primary motive is 'emotional', or even, irrational. In short, advertisers view their brands as products and their customers view brands as brands. If you accept that point of view it does have certain consequences. These are that while it is generally understood in the marketing industry that effective advertising – and in particular effective advertising strategy – should have a blend of 'emotional' and 'rational' characteristics, as a rule that balance is wrong.

LIES, DAMNED LIES, AND RESEARCH

It is here that you may well say that consumer research can play a part in getting the balance right between product and brand values, and so it may. Up to a point. For the fact is that research and advertising are unhappy bedfellows, and the preponderant belief in the advertising community is that research is the enemy of good advertising – whatever that may be – rather than the reverse. This is regrettable because if it is used at the right time, conducted by the right people, and sensitively interpreted by those aware of what it can and cannot do, it positively promotes the cause of – if not good – then at least effective advertising. It takes two basic forms:

1 research intended to help develop advertising;
2 research intended to assess its impact once it is in the field

A more dubious form that is supposed by some to predict how finished advertising will work has been enjoying a comeback over the past two or three years. This is discussed in chapter 7.

Research on strategy clearly falls into the first category (that intended to help develop advertising) and is useful. It normally takes the form of qualitative research, in which representatives of the target for the advertising – individually, in pairs, or in groups of six or eight – are interviewed by an experienced research 'moderator'. Given that it is the job of the advertiser and the agency to speculate in the first instance what sort of advertising message is *likely* to cause consumers to revalue, reassess etc., actually asking consumers themselves about these issues clearly can help. Both parties – the advertiser and its agent – tend to go into this sort of research with fairly clear preconceptions about what consumers think and feel about the brand and its advertising, and both parties are often surprised. By definition, neither the producer nor the advertising agent see things from the same point of view as the consumer. This means that the research can, theoretically, provide

arguments, propositions and strategies that between them agent and advertiser have overlooked; it can support arguments already voiced; and it can
rule out others that seemed to be front-runners.

However, you do have to remember *exactly* what this sort of research tells
you. Superficially it appears to be saying that if a given argument or message
was used in the advertising, this is how the target would react. Although this
may be the case, it is not, in fact, terribly likely. The research situation is a
highly artificial one in which consumers debate, discuss, consider and intel-
lectualise brand choice in a manner really rather remote from the cut and
thrust of the supermarket checkout. This, in the first instance, qualifies the
results. The second point is that the method requires consumers to predict,
or hypothesise about, their behaviour in the light of certain information. As
a moment's thought will suggest, few people display any great accuracy in
such areas, perhaps because we are all less rational in our actions than we
sometimes like to imagine. That means that this research method doesn't tell
you how people would react if they saw the proposed message in a piece of
advertising, or indeed in advertising repeated over two or three years; it tells
you how they react in focus groups. Doubtless these things are related;
equally clearly they are not the same thing. On the basis of a fair amount of
personal experience with this sort of research, I would say that it is my own
belief that consumers' responses to strategic material – messages about
brands – are close enough at least to provide a *useful guide* to how they are
likely to respond to such messages in advertising. As chapter 7 suggests,
their response to creative material seems less reliable.

STRATEGIES FOR THE 1990s

So far this talk of strategy has been general, making points about developing
strategies for brands that would, hopefully, make sense at any time. However, we are now in a particular time. Are there particular strategies appropriate for such a time generally, and recession and its aftermath particularly?
Every age has its spirit, and advertising as an ephemeral medium might be
thought to reflect and exploit this.

The point is, rather, that although advertising should indeed do just that,
advertising strategy should not. This is because strategy should be closely
related to brand strategy or positioning, and this in most instances should be
something relatively permanent that can always be said about the brand.
Thus, although a particular creative vehicle or idea may accurately and very
effectively explore the topical, because the strategy should reflect more
permanent brand values, it almost certainly shouldn't. This means that –

given that in the west the recession doesn't turn into a slump – an advertising strategy reflecting the currently relatively harsh economic circumstances does not necessarily make sense. This argument appears to be supported by consumer behaviour. Faced with significantly reduced total and disposable incomes, it might be supposed that consumers would either trade down to cheaper brands or buy their regular ones less frequently. As figure 5.5 suggests the evidence in the UK is that the tendency lies very much towards the latter. From a marketing point of view this is important. If there existed a significant level of trading down it might well make sense, even if temporarily, to reposition a brand towards a cost or value proposition. As this is not the general trend it would be unwise to do so. The brand may well be being bought precisely because its values remain unchanged, even in tough times. To tailor it unduly to prevailing circumstances could be to rob it of its appeal to existing purchasers.

Now, whether advertising strategy should reflect more underlying changes is another matter. It is, of course, a fact that – irrespective of recession – the west is becoming both a richer and an older society. It is also a society whose values are changing, such issues as health and the environment being further up the agenda in many countries than they were ten years ago. And it is even imagined in some quarters that the 'materialism' and 'consumerism' of the 1980s is being replaced by more socially conscious and responsible attitudes in the 1990s. Here the most important thing is to distinguish fiction from fact. The essence of effective strategy is that a brand at the very least maintains its position in a continuously changing world. Or to put it more simply, most brands have to change with the times and advertising is often the best way of ensuring that that's seen to be taking place. However, there's a distinction to be drawn between changes in consumer attitude that are actually taking place, and those that people paid to speculate – and that often means advertising agencies – might imagine to be occurring. Yuppies and Dinkies are no longer fashionable acronyms, but it doesn't follow that there aren't plenty of young, aspirational and – reasonably – affluent people around, with or without kids. Similarly, the hard evidence that the 'selfish' 1980s have been replaced by the 'caring' 1990s, and that behaviour is changing to match, is limited. Although it is crucial for brands to move with the times, and advertising is a good way of signalling this, it is equally important that strategy should be based on genuine, long-term and deep-seated changes rather than the ephemeral or imagined.

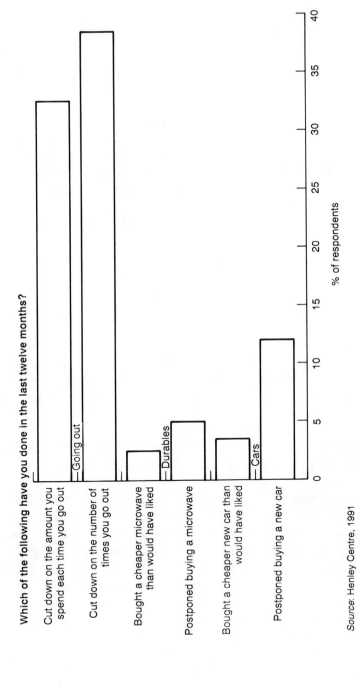

Source: Henley Centre, 1991

Figure 5.5 Consumer behaviour in the recession

TONE OF VOICE

You've now decided – or helped your agency decide – what the advertising should say and to whom it should be saying it. The final thing to consider then is how, tonally, you say it.

Tonal guidelines normally take the form of strings of adjectives like exciting, vibrant, youthful, considered, sober, formal, bold, newsy, fun. It's clear enough that not all of these are equally appropriate to every brand, message, and target. An ad for the local mausoleum would generally be ill-advised to adopt a tone which was youthful, newsy and fun. Similarly, while banks generally like to be portrayed as sober, responsible institutions, a note of fun *is* generally introduced into advertising trying to recruit young customers. Guidance for the creative department then is certainly helpful here, and perhaps the surprising thing is the limited extent to which tone of voice is thoroughly thought through or, even, experimented upon. It is a 'rule' of British lager advertising that the ads have to be funny. Why? Because all the other ads are funny. Is this now the only way of advertising lager? Nobody knows. Similarly, AIDS is a serious subject. So, naturally enough, the best way to persuade people to take preventive measures is to treat the matter seriously. Right or wrong? Nobody knows. This is an exaggeration, but it is certainly true that far more time is spent on establishing the right message for the advertising than the tone of voice, yet of the two the latter may be just as important in actually influencing what people think, feel and, perhaps, ultimately even do.

In practical terms, the tone of voice used should depend on three things:

- the nature of the brand;
- the nature of the message;
- the nature of the target

Brands have intrinsic qualities or values that the tone of voice should generally duplicate or complement; the message and its manner of expression should normally be in sympathy; and the tone should suit those who the ads are talking to.

CASE HISTORY 3
How to change the world

In summer 1990 those ad-men still in work and not on holiday in St Tropez were wondering what on earth Howell Henry Chaldecott Lury were doing using images of social prejudice to flog Fuji film. A radical young London agency with a clear taste for publicity, this instance suggests that they knew quite well what they were up to.

Fuji's problem was the familiar one of a market leader in its home country – Japan – finding the going tougher abroad, fighting particularly against the generic Kodak. Thus, in the UK, Fuji had a good reputation among professional photographers, but needed to widen its appeal among the growing number of amateurs who wanted to do more than simply record an event, and were using increasingly sophisticated equipment to do so. The requirement in marketing terms was to position Fuji as the professional quality film, thus appealing to aspirant amateurs.

This is a fairly typical advertising problem in that it offers no very immediate solutions – there was little to be said about the brand, the product or the people who used it that offered a very distinctive advertising strategy. The brand was familiar, and in general terms a good contender, but not number one; the product was comparable to the competition, with no outstanding qualities; the target similar. Other marketing variables – price, distribution – weren't major issues, and there was no opportunity to outspend the competition.

The strategic solution was clever. It eschewed the obvious, for example making a mountain out of a molehill of a product point-of-difference or using personality endorsement, and took as its starting-point the notion that photography is a medium that can make powerful impressions on people. The idea then was to create images which confronted popular preconceptions and prejudices, using the pay-off that Fuji – by 'making the best film we can' – enabled photographers to 'change the way people think'. The ultimate implication was that by using Fuji film you too can change the world.

The campaign comprised two 30-second TV commercials. The first showed shoppers' disparagement of a mentally-handicapped supermarket assistant, trumped by a check-out girl's friendship. The other showed an Asian woman shunned by mothers collecting their children from school; but as she hugs her child, a white girl looks on smilingly. Both freeze-framed the end-shot, the voice-over proclaiming that 'a photograph can make you see things differently'.

In depicting situations quite far from the idealised hyperbole of most advertising these commercials broke new ground, and were predictably controversial. There is also strong evidence that they worked. During the campaign period, spontaneous advertising awareness doubled, spontaneous brand awareness grew 37 per cent, and 'intention to purchase' doubled. In the realities of the market-place, Fuji's share grew by 50 per cent and its sales outperformed the market by 73 per cent. The other marketing variables were effectively static.

This is all good evidence that if you want to change the world, an imaginative strategy is a good first step.

CHECKLIST

1 Leaving aside specialist forms like direct response, it is useful to think of advertising taking four basic forms: it creates awareness, it challenges prejudices, it reinforces existing points of view, or it entertains. Developing an advertising strategy involves deciding which one the brand requires.

2 It also involves isolating a primary target audience for that message, because the message for one target won't necessarily be right for another. Much advertising is insufficiently focused on a particular group.

3 In defining the target it is often necessary to contrive segmentations tailored to the peculiarities of the particular market, rather than conventional ones.

4 Good advertising strategies should accurately reflect why people buy a brand, should say something unique about it, should be relevant to the target, take long-term positions, be single-minded, and be susceptible to dramatisation.

5 In practice, strategies often seem excessively oriented towards the product, at the expense of the consumer and the brand. Consumer research can be a practical and cost-effective method of helping redress this balance.

6 Advertising strategies should generally ignore short-term economic phenomena and concentrate on expressing long-term brand values.

7 Consideration of tone of voice is often neglected at the expense of the message, yet consumer response may be determined as much by the former as the latter.

6 THE GOOD, THE BAD AND THE UGLY
Briefing creative work

Pass it on! We're going to advance – Parson's on! We're going to France – Pass her on. We're going to dance – Lances on. We're taking the chance!

The creative multiplier · why briefing matters · five keys to better briefing · creatives are human · the written brief

Although it sometimes seems that a surprising number of people in marketing and even advertising still think otherwise, the creative work itself is the be-all and end-all of the advertising process. The sophistication of the strategy, the aggression of the media buying and the diplomacy of account handling all count for nought if on the day the ads themselves and the ideas behind them aren't up to scratch. The ad is the only visible expression of the time, trouble, thought and effort put into the whole process of advertising, the tip of the iceberg, the quintessence of the thinking of – perhaps – hundreds of people over – sometimes – thousands of hours of what the brand is all about. Only the work counts.

Obvious though this may be, as a fact it has several implications which are sometimes ignored. First, it might reasonably follow that – given their importance – as much time as possible should be devoted to developing the ads. Would that this were so. Too much time is idled away by advertisers and their agencies on peripheral matters divorced from the business of giving the creative department a clear brief and letting them get on with it. This is an organisational and management issue. The intellectual one is that of briefing. Advertisers don't invariably give their agencies brilliant briefs, and these are passed on, often with interest, in an elaborate game of Chinese whispers, to the agency creative department. The consequence is simple. The limitations of the material put into the department are more than accurately reflected in the material produced. Then, even if the ads themselves *are* satisfactory, agencies are often indifferent and advertisers no better at judging work. Add to that the deficiencies of the pre-testing techniques that are currently commonplace, then it sometimes seems surprising that any effective work ever sees the light of day. Improving the creative development process – or encouraging your agency to do so – thus follows the settling of the matters of targeting, the message and its tone of voice in the business of getting better advertising.

THE HOLY GRAIL

Creativity is the heart of the advertising business because it is potentially a multiplier of the advertising sum invested. Although the impact of the campaign will partly depend on how motivating the message is and how good a match is achieved between the target audience and the media selected, the chief factor governing impact is the creative idea. 'Multiply' is then a good term because it suggests that the idea can increase by a certain factor the effectiveness of the money spent; and, as has been remarked elsewhere, that factor can perhaps be up to fifteen. This matters because it distinguishes creativity from the other two advertising processes of strategy development and media placement. No one really doubts that the better the strategy and media work, the greater will be the impact of the campaign. Equally, few would claim that clever strategic or media work can *multiply* the effect of the money spent. Received wisdom is that this is exactly what good creativity can do, and while received wisdom – particularly in advertising – should always be regarded with suspicion, there's a reasonable amount of evidence that this is in fact the case. It's certainly true, for instance, that, dollar for dollar, some campaigns are four or five times more *noticeable* than those for comparable brands in the same market-place. This is a fact. Whether they are four, five, ten or fifteen times more effective is – inevitably – hotly debated. Empirical evidence suggests that in some cases they are. Creativity works. This is why it is marketing's holy grail.

PLACING THE ORDER

Bearing in mind the importance of the creative work, giving the creative people a full and accurate idea of what you and your agency have agreed the advertising needs to be and do, namely the strategy, matters and matters quite a lot. Doing this involves two things: face-to-face meetings, and the preparation of a written brief. This painfully simple point is worth making because there are still one or two agencies that perpetuate the absurdity of restricting the briefing process to the written brief alone. This ensures absolutely that the brief will be misunderstood.

Briefings, in any case, concern something about which agencies are paradoxically poor: communication. As difficult as it is for advertisers to put themselves in the position of consumers, so too is it often difficult for account people talking daily to their clients to put themselves in the position of creatives. Facts about the brand, the product and the prejudices of client management commonplace among the liaison people are by no means so to creative departments, which tend to work on a multitude of brands and projects, and are divorced from frequent contact with advertisers. Effective briefing accordingly requires of the briefers an imaginative act which goes beyond writing a few points down on a piece of paper, and at its best involves really conveying what consumers feel about the brand concerned, and how the advertising is intended to influence those feelings. The best way of achieving this is to ensure that the agency works in the following way.

1 It should take the creatives to the retail environment/shop in which the brand is sold. This is a way of forcing the people who have to try to sell the product to appreciate the perspective of purchasers. The very experience of, say, visiting a supermarket and trying to find a particular brand dramatises the point that there are an awful lot of brands out there clamouring to be bought, many of which look, feel and are priced pretty much the same.

2 It should give the creatives examples of the product and its competitors. All too often creative departments seem to be asked to sell airy nothings rather than objects – telephones, vacuum cleaners, condoms, bicycles, shoes – with quite distinct physical properties and identities. As far as possible the products should also be sampled.

3 Make sure you brief the creatives yourself. Agencies may not and probably will not agree with your perspective as an advertiser. But, whether they like it or not, that point of view has to be taken into account. As an advertiser you can offer insights into products and brands that agency personnel cannot invariably make themselves. And the process involves you in something which you are, after all, paying for.

4 Ensure the creatives are shown as much historical and competitive advertising as possible. It is important that they should have seen past work done on the brand. After all, consumers have. And it is equally useful for them to see how other agencies tackle comparable problems on competing brands.

5 Make sure they are given a proper written brief and taken through it.

Other than the invoice, the written brief is the most important single piece of paper an agency produces, and as such it is worth spending some time getting it right. Some, of course, aren't, because their authors don't concentrate sufficiently on remembering who they're writing for and with what end in view. The good brief is one that inspires the creatives to produce the advertising everyone has decided the brand needs. It has no other purpose. It is not a resumé of the problem the brand faces, with its strengths, weaknesses and the various competitive threats. It doesn't simply recount who consumes the brand, how many of them there are and where they live. It is, rather, something that sets in stone – or at least type – precisely what creatives need to know about the brand's problems, and the solutions envisaged. And absolutely nothing more. That is, beside the fact that it will encourage them to feel that, among the various briefs on their desk, this one summarises a problem that's particularly worth solving. It inspires. Creatives are human beings, too.

Naturally enough there is no ideal formula for writing a creative brief; and indeed the strength of the brief will often depend as much on *how* it is written as *what* is written. Still, there are a number of things that it's important to cover off.

1 Why are we advertising? This section spells out the threat to, or oppor-tunity for, the brand that normally prompts you as an advertiser to put your hand in your pocket. This might be to make people aware of the availability of a new product, or to support the premium quality of a brand in the face of a competitive product newly available at a cheaper price. More specifically, it is likely to be to inform, challenge, reinforce or entertain etc., in some particular way.

2 Who are we talking to? As has been suggested elsewhere, what really matters here is less where people live and how old they are, more how they go about buying brands in the given sector, and what they think and feel about the brand that is going to be advertised.

3 What do we want them to think, feel or ultimately do? This is another way of looking at what we want the advertising to do. State the single most important response that seeing the ad on the campaign is intended to elicit: 'I'd no idea that there was a new branch of Anne Summers open'. For the purposes of creative briefing it is important to decide here on the major response you need to get, even though subsidiary responses – 'I must pop down there and buy something for the wife' – will probably be carried. The limited nature of the advertising medium means that it is only effective when it concentrates on conveying a single message. This section is normally defined as the 'desired consumer response.'

4 How are we going to do it? This is the heart of the thinking on the brand and the essence of the advertising strategy. If you're going to inform, what are you going to say? If you're going to challenge . . .

CREATIVE BRIEF

Client: **Bass**	Product: **CBL TV**	Creative Team:
Job No:	Date: **8 November 1991**	Medium: **TV**

Background
Carling Black Label is the country's best-selling lager with a very strong base in the Midlands and North. It is being challenged – particulary in the South – by younger brands like Castlemaine and Fosters; whilst Heineken and Carlsberg continue to challenge nationally. The brand has long been supported by a very popular ad campaign – in a sector in which advertising plays a key role in influencing consumer choice. We need a new ad in the series.

The Product
Carling Black Label on draught and in cans. This is a top quality standard lager slightly stronger (4.0% ABV) than the majority of the competition.

Why are we advertising
  i) To sustain advertising and brand awareness.
 ii) To improve the image of the CBL product, and that of the people who drink it.
iii) To create goodwill towards the brand by maintaining a very high standard of original and enjoyable advertising.

Target Audience
– Younger lager drinkers: 18–24 C1/C2 . . . computer operators, telecom engineers, policemen and gas-fitters.
–Sardonic and cynical – with a functioning brain and wide frame of reference. Into music, clubbing, cinema, TV and football; talk (specially to each other) in irony and black humour – if it moves, take the piss out of it.
–Socially active; might have a regular local, but really drink at a repertoire of outlets – clubs, city bars, leisure centres, etc.

The Argument
The basic thinking behind the 'I bet he' campaign is that: 'Carling's a little bit special. You can tell by the people who drink it.' Which is to say that the ads depict an extraordinary, spectacular and very filmic feat, and observers then deduce – comment – that because the hero has demonstrated he's a special person, he must drink Carling Black Label.

Proposition
'I BET HE DRINKS CARLING BLACK LABEL'

Tone of Voice
In certain areas CBL is regarded as slightly old-fashioned and downmarket. Tonally we have to counter this.

Desired Consumer Response
'That's another great ad for Carling'.

Creative Requirements
A 40′ TV script which follows the basic formula but presents the brand in a rather more contemporary manner than some of the previous executions.

Your Reward
Fame and fortune that has traditionally come to the creators of Carling Black Label ads.

Figure 6.1   A summary example of a creative brief

5 What's a summary of this thinking in a single phrase? All too often this section – the proposition – is the only part of the brief that creatives read; and even if it is not, it is supposedly the verbal expression of a great deal of thinking.

6 What justifies this phrase? The answer is a list of evidence – rational, emotional, objective, subjective – that supports this idea. This is always useful, although it somehow suggests that consumers view advertising rationally. On the whole they don't, much apparently effective advertising simply taking the form of assertion.

7 What tone of voice should the advertising use? As has been suggested, the tone in which things are said is sometimes as important as what is said, and it is crucial that the manner of expression should be suited to the brand, what you need to do with it and the advertising's target.

8 What media should be used? This is a relatively complex issue related to the budget, the target, the brand and the message to be put across. It is enough here to specify requirements – TV, press, posters etc. They may or may not be accepted by the creative department.

9 Any other business. Other considerations will include the importance of developing existing work; the importance of abandoning all reference to existing work; the need to include coupons, response telephone numbers, government health warnings etc.

Providing it is well written it does not matter who writes this piece of paper. However, it does matter that it is agreed both within the agency and with you as the advertiser. The former will normally take place as a matter of course; the latter not necessarily. If you aren't formally committed to the solution the agency envisages, you are not very likely to be happy with its creative expression.

A summary example of a creative brief for Carling Black Label lager is shown opposite.

CHECKLIST

1 **Getting the creative idea right is the most important task in advertising development because of the potential strength of the creative idea. Creativity is a multiplier that can double, triple or quadruple the impact of the advertising spend – perhaps more.**

2 **Briefing creative departments on the sort of work a client needs is often superficially conducted. Creatives need to be as familiar with the brand, its**

consumers, its retail environment, client views and competitive ads as they are with the written brief.

3 This is not to denigrate the written brief. This should be a very rare beast. Namely a trenchant distillation of precisely what the creative department needs to produce the right work. And no more.

4 Make sure you see and agree with a piece of paper – the brief – that some agencies treat as an internal document.

7 TWELVE ANGRY MEN
Developing and judging creative work

The reasonable man adapts himself to the conditions that surround him.
The unreasonable man adapts conditions to himself. All progress depends on
the unreasonable man.

GEORGE BERNARD SHAW

*Creative judgement · barriers to good judgement · criteria · criteria to ignore ·
encouraging agencies to develop work · the perils of creative research ·
quantitative pre-testing · progress and the reasonable man · creative strategies
for the 1990s*

The work having been briefed, a period of intense silence ensues while the
creative department studies the brief, thinks up ideas, ponders other briefs
and goes out to lunch. For those outside the department on major projects
this is a time of intense concern and speculation; and it is equally so on the
part of the advertiser. Bonuses and promotions, if not careers, are at stake.
When, finally, and almost invariably late, the white smoke is spied over the
Vatican, you now face the single, most difficult job in producing good
advertising, which is trying to decide if the work's right. Not very many
people are very good at this.

This is partly the advertising industry's own fault. Often careless of
training people to the standards of professions with which it would presumably wish to be compared, it can be poor at what might be regarded as
the fulcrum of the empirical approach to advertising – providing feedback to
anyone, particularly creatives, on whether or not and how well their ads
work. If this did happen on a more regular basis, everyone would gradually
acquire a bank of experience based on the *actual impact on consumers of the
work*. As things stand, the experience garnered focuses less on the regular
responses of consumers to ads and more on those of advertisers. This is fine
in so far as unless the advertiser approves the ad the consumer won't see it
anyway. But it is obviously not ultimately a very good way of gradually
improving the quality – by which is meant the impact – of the work.

This isn't the only problem. If there's an occasional tendency to be careless of the ultimate target of advertising, then the blame has to be apportioned by saying that agency creative departments concern themselves rather too much with aesthetics, and agency account management are too concerned with their clients.

To take these points in turn, the creative award system that operates in Europe, the US and elsewhere sometimes seems in certain respects the enemy of effective advertising. This is quite simply because the criteria by which creative awards are given are purely aesthetic, and there is far from a proven correlation between advertising that looks good, entertains and makes people laugh, and advertising that works. As has been suggested, it is useful to think of advertising working in four basic ways. Of these approaches, one is indeed defined as what can be considered the aesthetic approach to advertising, which argues that the ad works as a self-contained entity, judged by its audience on aesthetic criteria, and saying little explicitly about the brand, other than that the advertiser is the sponsor of this attractive creation. In so doing it entertains, attracts viewers and wins their goodwill. The problem is then that while *some* advertising does indeed appear to work in that way, not all of it does. The snag with this is that creatives continue to aspire to awards, and judge their own and others' work by these aesthetic criteria. Indeed, they are promoted on this basis.

Account management is in some respects equally guilty, but in a different way. It is understandable that its chief concern should be the client's response to the work, but it is not ultimately excusable. To concern yourself with what your clients are likely to think and feel is certainly to ensure that they get what they want, but it doesn't necessarily follow that they will get what they need. And although they'll be pleased in the short term they may be less so in the long run. As a rule, agencies do know better than advertisers what they – the advertisers – need. Assessing creative work on the basis of whether the marketing director will like it or not is thus, in the long term, not a very good idea.

This points the finger clearly in the direction of advertisers themselves, the agency saying being that clients get the work they deserve. This is fair enough in so far as if agencies aren't themselves invariably brilliant judges of work, advertisers are generally no better. This is – perhaps – partly for a reason already explained. Working for Nabisco, Reuters, Cable and Wireless, the Bundesbank or Swires inevitably involves a degree of commitment to the company, its products and its prejudices, and that works against seeing a brand steadily, seeing it whole, and seeing it above all through the eyes of consumers: through a glass darkly. Equally there is much in any marketing job that is minimally to do with advertising, judging advertising ideas being a small – yet quite important – part of the task. Finally, there is little in any advertising that doesn't end up in some way being an expression of corporate self-perception. Companies and the people working for them need to think well of themselves, and their advertising is often the most public expression of the company's sense of itself. This sounds all well and good, but in practice it sometimes is not. Most companies like to see themselves as efficient, successful, happy and on the way up – and they very often want a sense of this reflected in their advertising. Now, if the company's brand itself needs to be seen *by consumers* as efficient, successful, happy and on the way up, everyone will be content. Yet that's far from invariably the case. There may well be a positive virtue in presenting a brand as gutsy, workmanlike, and populist. Here, where corporate aspirations are at odds with required brand personality, it is sometimes very difficult to get senior management – particularly outside the marketing discipline – to sign off work. And quite often corporate personality will indeed be at odds with that of the brand.

QUESTIONS OF JUDGEMENT

Despite these difficulties, it is, of course, necessary to try to make a thoughtful, informed and responsible assessment of the object on which so much money is spent, the creative work. Asking yourself the following questions may help.

1 Is it on brief?

One of the purposes of establishing a brief in the first place is to check the work against it when it is ultimately produced. This seems a straightforward enough business, but is in fact less so than it might at first appear. Creative work shouldn't simply mirror the brief because if it does it is not likely to be particularly 'creative' in the sense of imaginative. To use a familiar idea, the creative process is the alchemy which, at its best, turns the base metal of the brief into gold. It takes what is often a sufficiently prosaic proposition – say 'contentment' – and turns it into a campaign like 'Happiness is a cigar called Hamlet', one of the most popular campaigns in Britain for the last twenty years. In so doing it captures the consumer's imagination, and indeed as a slogan enters the language in a manner that epitomises the power of very good advertising. This means that good creative work is less a reflection of the brief than an interpretation of it.

Now this, in itself, challenges our judgement because we are likely to have to decide whether good work is a lively interpretation of the brief or, more simply, off brief. So evaluating the work isn't simply a question of ticking off the boxes and ensuring that the advertising objectives, strategy, desired response, advertising proposition and rational support etc. have all been covered off. Indeed, it is highly unlikely that *each* of those requirements will be equally well met by what should be a simple, single-minded, creative idea. Perhaps the best way of expressing the requirement is to say that if the letter of the brief matters relatively little, it is vital that the work captures its spirit.

2 Is there an idea?

Anything that actually *does* capture that spirit is likely to have an idea. Ideas are probably easier to recognise than define, and a good deal of paper has been wasted trying to do just that. For practical purposes, though, it is perhaps useful to say that an idea should be considered as a visual or verbal expression that combines distinctiveness with novelty. Thus, George Orwell's phrase 'All animals are equal' is an idea because it surprisingly confers on animals a right not enjoyed by all humans. Similarly, the Georges Pompidou Centre in Paris presented an idea, novel to the general public at the time, of putting its working parts – wiring, air-conditioning, sewerage etc. – on the outside of the building, rather than the inside.

That said, there are ideas and advertising ideas, and it is your job as judge both in the first instance to recognise – and congratulate – an idea, and in the second to try to decide whether it is an idea, or an idea related to the commercial purpose of selling the brand. Ideas matter because it's only by virtue of having an idea that the attention and imagination of the customer is going to be captured. Equally, the idea has to be expressive of or related to the brand in question. Putting money behind what is simply and solely an *idea* rather than an *advertising idea* puts the advertiser in danger of having the ad remembered, but not the brand the ad was supposedly promoting. In the best advertising, the idea is often intrinsically related to the brand – for instance the UK work for Benson and Hedges Silk Cut cigarettes. Here, the idea is the simple one of literally expressing the brand name: pieces of silk, cut by different instruments in different ways. Conversely, it has always been said that viewers of the long-running Cinzano TV campaign starring Leonard Rossitter and Joan Collins weren't sufficiently sure that the advertised brand was Cinzano rather than its rival Martini. Or was it the other way round?

3 Is it the right idea?

If you do feel you've recognised an advertising idea, you then have to be sure that it's the right one.

Right though doesn't imply only, because at any given moment there will be tens if not hundreds of perfectly satisfactory solutions to an advertising problem. What the word does mean is right for the brand, right for the objectives of the advertising and right for the consumer. Unless the advertising task is radically to change brand values, that advertising idea is likely to need either to be accurately expressive of the brand's current values, or closely related to them. This is, of course, why young stars like Michael Jackson and Michael J. Fox are used to promote Coca-Cola and Pepsi, rather than elderly eccentrics with connotations of the macabre like Peter Cushing and Christopher Lee.

This is obvious enough, but it needs to be qualified by the point that in some circumstances the brand may have to correspond to the idea as much as the idea to the brand. For instance, in Britain, identity was conferred on BarclayCard by the TV documentary presenter Alan Whicker. Advertising in this way often provides a meaning and value for brands which previously lacked them, and the question for the advertiser in these circumstances doesn't involve ensuring brand and idea fit. Rather, it means making sure that the idea is what, in due course, you want the brand to become. Thirdly, the idea should be right for the consumers or those consumers selected as the primary target. This again will seem obvious, but it is a point sometimes neglected. The same thing, idea, personality, or metaphor will often mean different things – sometimes diametrically opposed – to different people. So it is worthwhile considering whether the thing that you're using to represent the brand means to consumers exactly what you imagine it to mean. Allusions to *Paradise Lost* in an ad for a beer – a headline against an empty beer-glass – may or may not be appropriate to the target.

4 Is it a campaignable idea?

It is an old, true and often neglected saying that agencies and their clients tire of advertising long before consumers do. If brands are all about identities, and advertising is often the most powerful expression of that identity, then consistency of advertising is the best way of establishing the required meaning in the consumer's mind. Accordingly, when reviewing brand-building strategic ads, campaignability is crucial. This doesn't mean simply that the work can be repeated, rather that the idea is sufficiently distinctive to permit variations to be expressed over a period of time in which the original theme remains recognisable. This is, in fact, in itself a good test of whether there *is* an idea intrinsic to the work, or merely technique masquerading as an idea; or indeed no idea at all. An idea strong enough to merit the name will be capable of varied expression. If the campaignability of the idea is not immediately apparent, it is quite likely that the idea can't be so treated. Either way it is up to the agency to demonstrate the campaignability of the approach.

5 Is it a versatile idea?

The word versatility isn't used here in the same way as campaignability, but rather in the sense of being capable of being used in different media. Synergy – synchronised energy – or in advertising terms saying the same thing in the same way in different media – is another one of those ideas recognised but not much utilised in advertising. Its logic is manifest. In the same way as there is generally little point in saying all sorts of different things in different ways about the same brand in its packaging, sales promotional and advertising material, so too is there little mileage in inconsistent expression of the brand meaning in the different advertising media. Indeed, it is often simply a waste of money.

Of course it is true that certain ideas are far more suited to expression in one medium than another. An essentially visual idea can't readily be expressed in an aural medium like radio. Equally, an audio-visual idea might be expressible on TV and cinema, but not on posters. Admittedly, if the idea is of sufficient force in its main medium, it may well be entirely reasonable to accept running the same message expressed through a different creative vehicle in a subsidiary medium. However, as a rule, agencies are lackadaisical about this issue. While accepting the force of the argument, they sometimes don't actually go to a great deal of trouble to work a little bit harder and find ideas that *do* work across all media. In an ideal world they would, in any case, do more than that, with a visual or verbal identity spanning not only advertising but all forms of brand communication. There are some who argue that such versatility may lead to a lack of focus, since tight, vivid ideas are hard to translate across media. There's something in this, although it remains the case that agencies could and generally should try harder in this area.

6 Is it an understandable idea?

People who know what the ad's trying to get across occasionally fail to see the wood for the trees, not appreciating that what seems clear to them is far less so to the uninitiated: the consumer. Ads have to be comprehensible by those who know only what they say, not what they're trying to say.

7 Is it a different idea?

This is the seventh, the last and the most important question. It's easy for agencies to recycle old ideas and understandable that they should do so. The problem is that either people won't notice them, or else they will think that they are tired old ideas and so is the brand. This is undesirable. Freshness and originality is:

- more likely to be noticed;
- more likely to be remembered;
- more likely to imply something positive about the brand.

The best advertising ideas almost invariably break new ground in this way. True, they may be a fresh combination of familiar elements, but something about them *will* be fresh.

So much for the questions that should be asked. There are also one or two others that often *are* asked and shouldn't be.

1 Do I like it?

It is very difficult to escape from immediate, personal responses to advertising. They are also unlikely to be relevant. Bearing in mind the objectives set for the work – excite C2D housewives etc., – it is unlikely that the commissioner's aesthetic response matters very much one way or another.

2 Will consumers like it?

Again, an issue of debatable importance. The target needs to notice the ad in the first instance, get the message from it that the strategic work has deemed appropriate, and to some extent – probably – remember it. If they 'like' the ad this process may, possibly, be facilitated. Or it may not. No one appears yet to have firmly established a link between liking, remembering, acting, buying the brand by the case etc.; and although some advertising seems to work in this way, as has been suggested, not all of it does.

3 Will the MD like it?

This is a common question on the client side, but one which for obvious reasons, is to be very firmly set aside. Consumer response is the only criterion – or, rather, likely consumer response when the work is in the field.

PAINTING THE SISTINE CHAPEL

So you have now seen the first creative ideas and have applied – normally there and then – some thoughts, ideas, precepts and prejudices by way of coming to a judgement on them. The agency felt that the meeting went well – agencies always feel meetings go well – and an arrangement has been made to review the work in due course. It is now that it's often necessary to apply the whip hand. Agencies work quite hard to meet deadlines for creative presentations because it is the most important part of their job. The creative department is bullied, cajoled, bribed, threatened and pleaded with to produce some work and, normally, something is produced. All work now stops. The deadline has been met, the client is 'pleased' and there is another brief to be tackled. The problem with this understandable attitude is that creative work really does need to be developed, not just presented. If the agency actually *has* produced something recognisable as an idea, it has probably done quite well. Yet it is unusual for an idea in its nascent form to meet all, the majority, or even a minority of the various requirements normally laid down for an execution, let alone a campaign. Ideas do have to be tinkered with, developed, in certain cases transformed; in others abandoned. Yet having gone through all the trouble of giving birth, some agencies are far too exhausted by the labour to go through the process of ensuring that the idea achieves maturity.

There are two things to do to encourage them. The first is to take the work and actually consider, away from the pressures of the meeting whether it really stacks up. You should – of course – carefully consider all the questions listed above, but above all you should consider *whether the basic idea is right*. If it's not, the agency should be sent back to the drawing-board there and then. What happens too often is that the idea initially seems no more than adequate, and advertisers let themselves be over-persuaded by agency 'enthusiasm'. Concerns about the original idea subsequently resurface, and the whole thing is rejected very late in the day. If the idea is wrong – or rather, seems wrong – speak up soon. It is then up to the agency to persuade you, or even better demonstrate, otherwise. And this is a perfectly reasonable area of debate. Advertising is about trying to find a solution that comprises a highly succinct visual and verbal expression of something that is likely to have involved reams of paper and weeks, perhaps months, of debate. The proposed solution may well be a crucial stepping-stone in the process of you and the agency finding the correct solution. Creating an ad isn't the elegant and logical process of – say – ordering luncheon at Simpsons or Shepheards Hotel. It is a muddled and experimental process of trial and error in which, as J. Walter Thompson's sometime London chairman

Jeremy Bullmore acutely puts it, 'Only in the search for the solution will the true problem be fully recognised and understood.'

The second option is to threaten to research the work. This almost invariably galvanises agencies into action because agencies so dislike research. This is because it takes the power of creative judgement away from where it should rightly be – the agency – and places it purportedly in the hands of the consumer, but in practice in an equally unappealing alliance of the consumer and the researcher who 'interprets' the consumer.

Actually, certain sorts of research are, in some respects, helpful in developing creative work. The most useful is that which takes the same form as strategic research – getting an experienced researcher to show the crude ideas to the target audience, and seeing what they think of them. As has been suggested, this technique has its limitations – particularly because of the difference between what people say on the one hand; think, feel and later do on the other – and what it certainly doesn't do is to provide guidance on the entire range of things that ads generally need to do if they are to work. That is:

1 they need to be noticed in the first place (many aren't);
2 they need to be understood (not all are);
3 they need to say something relevant about the brand and relevant to the consumer (not all do);
4 they (probably) need to be (consciously) remembered;
5 they need above all to capture the imagination;

Qualitative research generally seems helpful in providing some sort of insight into the second and third of these five points: whether or not the ad is understood, and whether or not it seems appropriate for the user and the brand. For instance, in the case of the *Paradise Lost* ad mentioned earlier, research might reveal that the target were without exception *aficionados* of the poem and relished the allusion in the work; that they knew *Paradise Lost*, and abhorred the commercialisation of ecstatic poetry; that they'd never heard of *Paradise Lost* but got the point anyway; that they found the ad utterly incomprehensible; that they thought the comparison inappropriate for a brand of beer. This sort of information is useful.

Given that the audience is a captive one, this form of research is less instructive on the more important matters of noticeability, memorability and absolute appeal, so its use should depend on what the issues surrounding the advertising are. If there's serious doubt over whether the ads are expressing what everyone intends them to express, it is a good idea; if concerns surround the power or impact of the idea it's altogether less so. This is especially the case because 'impact' often gets confused with 'liking'.

Unpractised judges of advertising – respondents in qualitative groups – tend to judge ads by whether they like them or not. As has been remarked, this doesn't necessarily have much bearing on whether they will notice the ads on the side of a bus in six months' time and rush out to buy the brand as a consequence. Millward Brown, one of Britain's more experienced ad-tracking agencies states: 'It turns out to be much harder than anyone expected to predict real life communication efficiency. Most commercials we track have been assessed qualitatively: but there is little relationship between tracking study performance and the level of enthusiasm in the group discussion report.'

However, the reality is that few executions on which significant sums are spent these days escape some sort of consumer testing; and given the fact that the consumers are the people that are aimed at, this is in principle a good idea. The issue rather lies in the nature of the research, who does it and above all its interpretation. For creative development purposes the sensible approach is:

1 to do it;
2 to do it in a small-scale qualitative manner;
3 to use a highly experienced researcher familiar with creative development work (and not the junior partner);
4 to make sure that your agency briefs him or her fully about the brand, the target, and what you want the advertising to do.;
5 to focus its objectives on communication issues rather than those of the 'merit' of the idea;
6 To regard its results as a guide to how consumers may react, as opposed to a description of how they will.

The final step is then to make sure that the agency listens to the research findings and, if necessary, does something about them. You should then, at some altogether later date, have a campaign or an execution with which you and the agency are both reasonably happy.

HOW TO KNOW THE UNKNOWABLE

It is now that the horrible spectre of pre-testing looms. This is distinct from creative development research because it is normally conducted on more or less finished work, and because it focuses on the sort of things that qualitative work can't provide – measures of noticeability and stand-out. Pre-testing sometimes also seems to be being used to try to predict more generally whether the ads will 'work'.

The commonest form is a quantitative test in which the finished film is shown among competitive material, or a finished press ad in a folder or magazine. The audience is shown this material and is then asked which of the ads they can remember. Once these have been identified, more detailed questions are asked about the impression they made, what they were trying to get across and so on. As ever with testing, the problem is that these circumstances are rather artificial. As with its qualitative cousin, the audience is asked concertedly to examine, analyse, discuss and pass judgement on material among a bunch of strangers or in the presence of the questioner and the questionnaire. This is rather different to lolling in front of the television on a Saturday night, passively accepting ads and generally willing to be entertained by the material. It follows that – as with the qualitative test – while there's doubtless a relationship between responses in the pre-testing situation and those of seeing the film on air, here the relationship generally seems rather less close.

The research does, of course, provide some sort of large-scale measure of how noticeable the test ad appears to be by comparison with the others chosen, generally together with some indications as to what sort of message the testers are taking out of the ad, and some indication of the impact of the ad – in the test situation – on brand imagery. And these can be, and often are, compared with average performances. However, as no one has yet firmly established a decent correlation between pre-testing and what actually happens when the ad's on air, it's not entirely clear where this all gets you. It probably does add to the understanding of the nature of what has been created, and help you formulate hypotheses about how the work *may* operate in the field. The problem then is that it's sometimes used not for this entirely helpful purpose, but as an important contributor to the decision whether or not the ad should run – ads made for some advertisers that 'fail' to achieve average scores often don't run. This is really to ignore the general artificiality of the test situation, and also the important fact that much advertising has a cumulative effect derived from multiple exposures of the work over considerable periods.

It's probably worth adding that advertising at its most basic means drawing attention to things, and this quite often involves challenging the target's preconceptions and beliefs about given products and brands. By and large people are conservative, find this process unsettling, and would rather be left to their own devices, cosy in their own prejudices. It follows that the tendency in pre-testing is that – given the option as they are – consumers reject the radical, the uncomfortable and the surprising, and endorse more conventional expressions and creative vehicles. This can be a recipe for anodyne advertising. Effective advertising doesn't generally just reflect current consumer sentiment, thinking, or taste. It challenges, anticipates and attempts to mould it. The consequence of this is that although the pressure to ensure that advertising which is about to be put into production is 'right', the proliferation of pre-testing designed to achieve this isn't likely to achieve the effect desired – it tends to pander to the public's innate conservatism and in so doing can discount good ideas. As Paul Feldwick, planning director at Boase Massimi Pollitt/Doyle Dane Bernbach puts it:

Most advertisers would like to know, before they spend their advertising money, what effect the proposed activity will have on their business. Most punters would like to know, before they fill in their betting slip, which horse is going to win the 3.30 pm race at Haydock Park. Neither wish is unreasonable. However, because the wish is there it does not necessarily follow that a reliable method of prediction exists.

Together, these points suggest that the only really satisfactory form of pre-testing is post-testing: evaluating what the work is actually doing when it is in the field. You can only predict something once it has happened.

CREATIVE STRATEGIES FOR THE 1990s

The final point that you might well think about before signing off the work is the extent to which ads should be tailored to the times, and – more importantly – judged as such. In Chapter 5, the suggestion was that as the job of much advertising was to contribute to the brand's permanent values, it was unwise to be blown off course by – hopefully – temporary economic and social phenomena. Conversely, it was argued that the creative approach should be more flexible in adapting itself to the times.

The second point here is worth considering further. Earlier in the chapter, an effective advertising idea was defined as something that combined distinctiveness with novelty, and if you accept that definition then it follows that effective advertising ideas are likely to be highly contemporary. Individual advertising executions – as opposed to campaigns – are not expected to be anything other than ephemeral, and probably possess much of their power because they are latching on to contemporary slang, crazes, other advertising or news. In so doing they capture consumer imagination by exploiting, referring to, commenting on the contemporary scene, and become an attractively consumable part of daily life. Their strength is their novelty and contemporaneity. That said – that the advertising idea or creative expression should be contemporary – it by no means necessarily follows that it should be uniquely contemporary. Suited, that is, *only* to its own times. The best advertising often seems to combine the vividly contemporary with something rather more timeless; it marries the clothes of the time with the qualities that invariably attract people's attention. Those qualities are of course very varied, but all in some way affect or exploit the peculiar ways in which people think and feel. It follows that the best advertising – like the best films, novels or plays – exploit people's desire to be loved, frightened, thrilled, and so on. In this sense good advertising is a conventional art in that it imitates, reflects, highlights or parodies aspects of life. The best advertising often combines an ability to be thoroughly contemporary, while at the same time tapping the common thoughts and feelings to which people respond at any time. It is ultimately for this reason that very good advertising really is a money multiplier.

CHECKLIST

1 Judging creative work is the most difficult of the jobs facing either agency or client. It requires the judge to suppress any personal views, and imagine how consumers are likely to respond to work in the long term.

2 To help come to this judgement, questions to ask about the work include: is it on brief; is there an idea; is it an idea that is right for the job; is it campaignable, versatile and understandable? The question above all is, is it different?

3 Judging has to be followed by development. Agencies having presented the initial idea, can be lazy about progressing work and sometimes need to be encouraged by means of detailed and constructive criticism and, if necessary, creative development research.

4 Pre-testing of finished work is an understandable attempt to predict how consumers will react to finished work. Given the impossibility of the task, it is misguided and in certain instances is counter-productive.

5 There are no simple creative solutions peculiarly suited to the 1990s. The best creative work is both uniquely of its time and timeless.

8 FOR A FEW DOLLARS MORE

Getting better media value

'Now, Bertie, I want you to listen to me attentively. Are you there?'
'Yes. Still here.'
'Well, then, listen. I have at last succeeded, after incredible difficulty, and in face of all the evidence, in almost persuading Sir Roderick that you are not actually insane. He is prepared to suspend judgement until he has seen you once more. On your behaviour at Skeldings, there –'
'But I had hung up the receiver. Shaken. That's what I was. S. to the core.'

P. G. WODEHOUSE
Jeeves and the Yuletide Spirit

Unexciting but important · increasingly complex · the twentieth-century media explosion · history is bunk · the media target · choosing the medium · choice within media · media departments and independents · media briefing · better media value

With some sort of consensus being reached on the merit or otherwise of the creative work, consideration now turns to the detail of the medium in which it is going to be expressed, normally without a great deal of enthusiasm. The crosses in boxes which are the substance of most media presentations somehow lack the *élan*, the panache, the magic of the creativity, and the opportunity to form and express a personal opinion as to whether the work is right for the brand. Moreover, media often takes the graveyard spot in agency presentations, namely immediately after lunch. Many advertisers and agency personnel wish themselves, and often are, elsewhere. This is a pity because media is of course by far the largest cost associated with advertising, it is a subject of peculiar and daily increasing complexity, requiring quite high levels of both qualitative and quantitative judgement, and although it is far more difficult to get media wrong than creativity, it is the easiest thing in advertising to get it not as right as it should be. Accordingly, when you're looking for incremental improvements in advertising performance, media joins the other chief disciplines of strategy and creativity as an unholy trinity of concerns.

Getting it right – or getting it better – involves the established processes of settling on the media target, selecting the medium or media most effective in reaching that target, selecting titles or programmes within that medium, buying them and, sometimes, seeing if they've worked. Media planners and buyers need to understand these processes for obvious reasons; agency people outside media should be familiar with them because they are – or should be – an integral part of the advertising process; and advertisers should familiarise themselves with the business because it is their money that is being spent and agency practices usually need to be overseen. Many advertisers are also currently faced with the dilemma of continuing the conventional arrangement of letting the agency that is responsible for the creative work also buy the media, getting a media independent to do so, or adopting the compromise of centralising media-buying within a single agency, separate creative agencies furnishing creativity for the different brands. This is a more than legitimate issue as advertisers rightly seek better value for money. The danger is that cost will be misconstrued as value. Bulk buying discounts associated with centralised buying look highly attractive and, apparently, are quantifiable. Media, however, is by no means invariably a commodity that can be bought in bulk, the issue thus resolving into one of quantity versus the quality that is arguably achievable for a few dollars more.

THE MEDIA JUNGLE

It's worth starting with a definition and a glance at the current media scene. The media can be regarded as the conduit which link advertisers and consumers, the intermediary or middleman between the two groups, the place where ideas can be seen or, in the case of radio, the way in which they are heard.

Advertisers and consumers are both interested in the media but for significantly different reasons. For viewers, readers and listeners, they are ends in themselves as providers of information and entertainment. For advertisers, the media are rather means to the end of communicating with the people who consume the media. The public pays to be informed and entertained, primarily by the editorial material, while the advertiser pays to place advertisements supposedly incidental to the editorial in the hope – the anticipation – of being noticed by the public. Both public and advertiser directly or indirectly pay the media owner who therefore has two groups to keep happy. The public, who wish to be entertained; and the advertiser, who wishes to address particular people who may thereby ultimately be persuaded to buy something. The media owner delivers an audience to the advertiser by entertaining that audience.

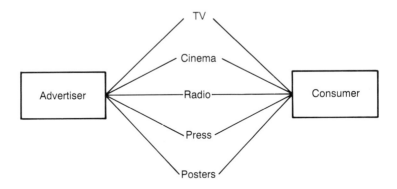

Figure 8.1   The media conduit

This definition is largely unaffected by the passage of time, yet from the media point of view the twentieth century has, in other respects, been one of quite a lot of change.

At the turn of the century print was really the only advertising medium, specifically posters, newspapers and magazines. Of course, as a medium, print presupposes a literacy that ninety years ago was by no means commonplace and is still short of universal in many countries – including Britain and the US – now. It was thus a way of communicating with the literate, who were in practice the privileged. The development of radio and cinema in the 1930s and TV in the 1950s represented progress of a sort because they were the first genuine mass-media actually reaching, and capable of communicating with, the majority of the population – because of course they used the spoken and not the written word. From the advertiser's point of view this represented a giant leap for mankind. At its simplest, you are not very likely to have a mass-market brand until you have a mass-market means of communication about that brand. In this sense national and international brands have been to an extent created by the availability of a means of communicating with national and international audiences. Of course, the mere fact that the medium is there doesn't mean it will be used, but in practice media consumption has grown in line with media diversification. Increasing media usage is also a function of time and money. Although interrupted by two world wars, the story of the industrial nations during this century has been one of increasing leisure time and increasing disposable income to spend on leisure pursuits. People these days can afford to buy televisions and now have enough spare time to watch them quite a lot.

The point of all this talk about the past is that it explains the present and to an extent influences the future. The position at present is that most countries have a very considerable diversity of media. As a consequence, all sorts of different people are consuming all sorts of different media, and thus the *basic media department job of matching the media bought to the media consumption habits of the brand's target* is relatively complex. The problem then lies in the fact that the job is going to become more rather than less difficult. This isn't because there's very much around that's new, rather because the forces for change that have shaped the present remain and will influence the future. Thus the technological development which has fuelled media diversification is very much continuing. It is doing so most obviously in the shape of satellite and cable television, which in penetration terms in most places is still limited. However, it would be naïve to assume it will remain so. The less glamorous aspect of technological evolution is the way in which it is bringing down the entry costs of creating new media. Hitherto it has been impossible to provide individual towns with their own television stations because the audience so derived was too small to meet the capital costs. But the cost in real terms of setting up radio stations, TV stations, newspapers and magazines is now falling quite rapidly. This means that the next few years are going to see not only a significant growth in local media, but also in niche media covering subjects that have too small a popular appeal to justify mass market coverage. Interesting though this doubtless is in its way, the key point lies in its implications. As has been suggested, the most prominent feature of the current media scene is its diversity and the difficulties for media planning that diversity poses. The consequence of the continuing growth of media is further diversity and, indeed, positive fragmentation. Consumers currently have considerable choice of media. That choice is going to increase. At the moment if you have a mass-market brand you can use a mass market-medium like television and a mass-market programme like a soap-opera to 'cover' or reach 10 per cent or 15 per cent of your target at a stroke. In ten years' time there may be no mass-media and no mass-market programmes. This will make reaching your target more difficult.

Finally, at the same time as the media themselves are fragmenting – concentrating on more specialised editorial matter for smaller audiences – it's also worth remarking that media ownership is being consolidated. The growth of the media, especially post-war, has meant that it is now very big business. According to the brokers James Capel, in 1990 there were forty-three international media companies with turnovers of more than $1.5 billion, the lot adding up to the grand total of $140 billion, equalling the GDP of the Netherlands. This is big business making lots of money and wanting to make lots more. So the paradox is that as the individual mediums, titles and programmes get smaller, they get bought up by larger and larger groups: control of the media is increasingly becoming concentrated into the hands of a relatively small number of major corporations. Like the process of media fragmentation, this isn't unequivocally good news for the advertiser.

Essentially, it shifts the balance of power between advertiser and media owner in favour of the latter, by limiting the advertisers' choice. The media owner knows that the advertiser wishes to reach a given target. This is covered by various titles and programmes. If the owner possesses the majority – even a significant proportion – of these, the advertiser is obliged to use them and media owners can charge more or less what they like. Market forces no longer prevail.

The consequence of all this is a situation of peculiar dynamism. With people's consumption of media changing perhaps more rapidly than ever before, it is incumbent on agencies to keep themselves – and you – abreast of it all. The best use of media will, clearly enough, involve a rapid recognition of changes in a brand's target's use of media and the exploitation of that opportunity.

MEDIA PLANNING AND MEDIA BUYING – A JOB DESCRIPTION

Still, the future is probably best left to take care of itself. The present normally offers advertisers sufficient problems, particularly by way of sorting out media for a campaign, preferably even getting it better.

The medium, then, is where the ad is placed. Given that different people consume different media – and different titles and programmes within those media – the media department job is to place the ad in the media, pro-grammes and titles used by people who you want to buy your brand. Superficially this simply involves two things:

- knowledge of the advertising target;
- knowledge of the target's use of media.

On this basis appropriate media and titles can be selected, and this is the basic job of *the media planner*. The business is complicated by the fact that the media then have to be bought, and a medium, title or programme that effectively reaches or covers the majority of a given target may be too expensive for the budget available. For example, if you've got only $50,000 to spend it's a mistake to splash out on a TV ad which most of your target will see, but which you can afford to screen only once. Media choices are therefore also a function of cost – and in the first instance official or 'ratecard' costs of the various media. The extent to which these are negotiable varies from medium to medium, time to time and, indeed, person to person, the person on whose bargaining skill you depend in this instance being the *media buyer*. The media process is therefore a trade-off between what a planner proposes as theoretically desirable in terms of a fair pro-portion of the target seeing the ad normally at least three times – technically the *frequency* – and what a buyer suggests is in practice affordable and, during any given period, available. In practice, media planner and media buyer are often the same Jekyll and Hyde person.

MATCHING AND MIXING

This all seems reasonably simple. It becomes less so when you begin to look at the component parts. The first of these is the target.

Most marketing activity legitimately targets everyone who is currently buying, or who might buy, a brand: for instance, for a soap-powder, all housewives; and for an everyday beer, all men. Such matters as packaging and pricing concern this total target, and it is not unreasonable that all these people should be taken into account when making packaging or pricing decisions. Whether they have to be taken *equally* into account is a different matter, but considered they must be. As has been suggested elsewhere, an *advertising* target is almost invariably smaller than a marketing target. This is partly because advertising budgets rarely allow such large targets to be effectively addressed – the butter's spread too thin; also because it is generally assumed that part of the marketing target is more important for advertising purposes than another. Thus, depending on what you're trying to do with the brand, some sort of targeting decision is generally made, for instance to address existing purchasers or target potential users: in terms of the groupings established earlier in the book, to 'reinforce' or to 'challenge'. This distinguishes the marketing target from the advertising target. And, of course, it may be differentiated in various other ways. Advertising can target lapsed users, it may try to persuade light users of a product to become heavy ones, etc., etc.

However, advertising as a term is itself being used imprecisely here. The 'advertising' target is in fact often divisible into three: the strategic target;

the creative target; and the media target. In most cases these will overlap, sometimes they will be entirely the same, but they are in any case still worth calling something different:

- The *strategic target* is the group of people we actually want the advertising primarily to address: say lapsed users of Nescafé, or existing users of a competitive brand. Demographically, these people are definable as housewives between the ages of 25 and 60.

- The *creative target* is normally a group within this group on whom the creative department should be asked to focus. You can't sensibly depict in a single TV commercial housewives between the ages of 25 and 60. As most people want to be younger than they actually are, creatives are normally asked to focus on housewives between 25 and 30.

The *media target* is something different again. It might be assumed that this was the same as the strategic target. Unfortunately, usually this isn't quite the case. The various media deliver – indeed are often designed to deliver – particular audiences. The problem is that these audiences don't normally correspond very closely to the strategic target you should have devised with your agency. It is not usually possible to buy time or space in media vehicles that deliver, say, lapsed users of a given brand of sanitary protection (sanpro) – or even Nescafé. It is entirely possible to buy larger groups within which such sub-groups are likely to be found, but that is not quite the same thing. Hence, unless you actually know the media consumption habits of the strategic target, the media target tends to be defined as a broader group, the media habits of which you *do* know, say all coffee users. The key issue here is clearly the existence or otherwise of comprehensive quantitative media research, and this varies very considerably from brand to brand, from product sector to product sector, and indeed from country to country.

The consequence of this is quite important. It means that one of the more important judgemental skills in the media planning/buying job involves minimising the wastage – people seeing ads not targeted against them – inherent in the whole process. This involves three stages:

1 deriving a media target from the strategic advertising target;
2 seeing what media these people consume, using quantified media research;
3 making more subjective judgements about whether these media/titles/ programmes suit the brand, its marketing and advertising objectives, and the particular ads.

This last stage is really crucial because it's here that the judgement, under- standing and expertise of the media people comes in, because it is they who should be able to make informed subjective judgements on such issues as what the *Hello!* reader is really like and whether it's really the right place for an ad for something as workmanlike as a mountain bike.

And yet it's equally here that the process can fall apart. For one reason or another, media people sometimes seem to be regarded as pariahs whose job – at short notice – is to jack up a media plan. This is self-defeating because the whole business of media-buying benefits enormously from the media department having an understanding not simply of who the advertising is trying to reach and which media they consume, but the problems the brand faces as a whole, the nature of the competition, the nature of the advertising, and the sort of qualitative understanding of consumer motivation that is the substance of advertising strategy. Thus, the first thing you can do as an advertiser to foster this process is to ensure that this sort of understanding on the part of the media people exits. And this is likely in itself to mean work on your part.

CHOOSING THE MEDIUM

Having settled the media target, the next thing is for you and the agency to discuss which of the media, or which combination, to use. The decision-making process here is relatively complex and can have far-reaching implications for the effectiveness of the work.

The first consideration – and in certain respects the last too – is the *media target*. National newspapers, national TV and national radio – if you have such a thing – will certainly deliver the lapsed sanpro user, but are unlikely to do so cost-effectively. Apart from anything else these media deliver men as well as women to the advertiser, and even though deft choice of programme, title and positioning will raise the proportion of women reached, the level of wastage is likely to be high. This is a waste of money, especially when 'women's titles' are likely to be available, some of which will be able to deliver not only a high proportion of women, but also a high proportion of pre-menopausal women, a small proportion of which are statistically likely to be be lapsed users of the brand.

Generally the next consideration – sometimes the first – is *cost*. Given that a brand has national distribution and – a different thing – needs national advertising support, it is not normally possible to produce a TV ad for less than a very substantial sum. This, of course, is a gross cost. The *cost-per-thousand* (cost of reaching a thousand people in your target, or CPT) achieved by TV is normally very good. But the very facts of its – usually – high penetration and high production costs debar many advertisers. They are then faced with the print media with lower gross costs, lower production costs, but in the case of the press, sometimes more limited penetration; and ultimately higher cost-per-thousand. Or radio, with very low production costs often matched with limited penetration.

Having sorted out the media target and determined what you really can afford to spend, you can now put together a table which shows how far your money will go against your target in the different media.

Table 8.1 How to spend a million dollars

	COVER	FREQUENCY
National Press	87	4.3
Television	75	3.6
Posters	61	20.3
Radio	55	15.6
Cinema	18	2.1

(These figures are for the UK, based on a target of all adults)
Source   WCRS

This analysis apparently solves the problem because it suggests that press is probably your best bet – you're covering almost 90 per cent of the target at a just about adequate level of frequency. In fact calculations of this nature are misleading in so far as they ignore a number of other considerations that also have to be taken into account. The first of these is the *differing impact of the media*. The best is perhaps cinema. This has all the advantages of television as an audio-visual colour medium, without the patent deficiency that TV, for many, is a background medium used to keep the kids happy rather than something to concentrate on. The ads are part of the cinema experience and the audience, free from distractions and out to be entertained, concentrates on them and takes them in. Conversely, although press lacks sound, movement and drama, it does have the ability to put across a detailed, verbal, rational message. Leaving aside high levels of wastage – everyone sees posters – billboards have all the limitations of press plus the need to be simple, immediate and direct. Radio, likewise, is limited, but by the fact that it is simply and solely an aural medium, so if you've got a great-looking product it is scarcely the medium to use.

It is also worth remembering that the *different media are used in different ways* in a manner by no means taken into account by cost-per-thousands arguments. For instance, research in the UK indicates that radio is a medium generally used to provide background entertainment while some other activity – driving, washing the dishes, having sex – is taking place. This is also true – though rather less markedly – of TV, where some research suggests that 60 per cent of the audience are also doing something else while watching. Conversely, reading a newspaper or magazine is a more active process on which the reader is obliged to concentrate. At least theoretically this has implications for the impact of ads. It's also true generally that knowledge of *how* media are being used by particular groups as opposed to *who* uses them it is often limited. This is increasingly being recognised as an important omission, and the more energetic media planners are beginning to do something about it. In practice this means complementing the quantitative data on who reads/watches what, with qualitative research. This can reveal that, keen though young mid-market male adults may be on television, they rarely watch it between 8pm and 11pm because it's then that they are out on the town; and that though they buy popular newspapers, they look at them cursorily, mainly to see what's on TV . . . This sort of information is patently useful and can make the difference between a good and a great piece of media planning.

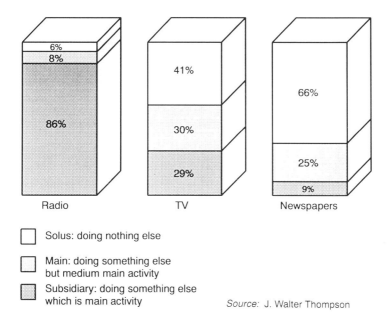

Figure 8.2 How the media are used

All this means that simple cost-per-thousands calculations have to be qualified by overlaying the strength of the medium and, often, how it is used by your target. You may be reaching people apparently more cheaply in one medium, but more cost-effectively in another. It is also, of course, true that the choice of medium should be significantly influenced both by *the nature of the brand and the nature of the message*. A brand the appeal of which is predominantly visual is no better advertised on radio than are hearing aids. Equally, a campaign the objective of which is simply and solely awareness may well very effectively use posters as the simplest of all media. Here the *creative department* – responsible after all for actually contriving the message that consumers will see – is likely to have fairly strong views on the suitability of the medium for the message. Neither are they the only people with opinions. The *'trade'* – retailers – are a body that it is normally important to keep sweet on the grounds that, in the absence of decent distribution, most brands have an uphill struggle. Most believe that advertising is synonymous with TV and that other media options don't count. These views do at least have to be taken into account. The same also has to be said of your *opinion as the advertiser*, and the received media wisdom of your department, which may be considerable. There's also the issue of *competitive activity*. Competitive brands often make similar media choices, arguably on the grounds that they have similar target audiences, similar brands, similar messages and similar spends. These aren't always good arguments if the essence of the advertising business is to stand out from the crowd – or to zig when the competition zags.

The final issue to determine in choosing the medium is not which one but which ones. Particularly when larger budgets are available, you can spread your activity across several media, and may well be best advised so to do. Whether you should and how you should will depend on the broad advertising objectives and the established media strategy. For instance, given the varying capability of the media, it may well be sensible to concentrate one message in one medium, and cover a complementary one in another. TV is good at dramatising a case for a given brand and sometimes demonstrating it. It's less good at providing substantiation for that case – this is normally a job for press. Equally, a tactical radio campaign can usefully support a promotion without the expense of a TV commercial. There are also the issues of coverage and frequency. Normally, media objectives are to achieve 'adequate' levels of coverage and frequency for a campaign, usually meaning that the media schedule ensures that the majority of the set media target sees a given execution a reasonable number of times – three is regarded as the minimum for TV, six for press, within a reasonable period. Now, despite its theoretical attractions, this requirement normally excludes using cinema as a lead medium on the grounds that people go to the cinema so infrequently it would take years to achieve decent levels of coverage and frequency. Cinema can thus usefully be added to the media mix if another lead medium is used to provide base levels of cover.

This sells vodka

Fuji changing the world

Another try

Who's read the poem and does it matter anyway? Qualitative research can help

Saying 'Aah' for Dequacaine. Trick photography scales new heights

SKIN CARE BY HEROIN.

Take heroin and before long you'll start looking ill, losing weight and feeling like death. So, if you're offered heroin, you know what to say.

HEROIN SCREWS YOU UP.

Why to say no, from the Department of Health

The first recorded use of sex to sell ice-cream.
Tastes good and jolly successful too

It takes up to 40 dumb animals to make a fur coat.

But only one to wear it.

LYNX

Fighting the fur trade

If you don't want animals gassed, electrocuted, trapped or strangled, don't buy a fur coat. P O Box 509 Dunmow, Essex Tel: 0371 2016

Sheer creativity by Lynx. Catalytic in the decline of the UK fur coat trade

Photo: David Bailey

It's finally worth saying in this context that the sum of the parts of an advertising campaign is undoubtedly smaller than its whole. Complementary, synchronised campaigns in different media very often appear to work better either than the same campaign in a single medium or complementary work used at different times.

So much for the criteria. What about actually making the choice – or making sure your agency makes the right choice? The best piece of advice here is that given that an awful thing does have to happen – a choice has to be made – it's really your job to ensure it's done for the right reasons. There are fairly logical procedures, as described, that should lead you and your agency to a sensible choice of medium. Make sure those prevail. For instance, agencies generally, and their creative departments particularly, greatly like the TV medium. It's glamorous, good for agency publicity and is often simpler – it's less likely to consume agency time than lots of press ads. You may also yourself think that it's rather exciting to be on TV. So it is. Is it, however, the best media choice? One of the problems with media planning is that as there are so many considerations to be taken into account the temptation is to take short-cuts and come up with easy options. This isn't the best use of your money.

CHOICE WITHIN THE MEDIA

Choosing the right media is thus a relatively complex business, and the same can be said of the second stage of the media planning process – selecting individual titles, radio and TV stations, sorting out time-lengths and print sizes, and taking a view on such issues as position.

Superficially, the first step – choosing a TV station or a series of titles – couldn't be simpler. The media that the target audience consume are ranked in terms of how much each costs to reach a thousand of the target. Given that a particular title or programme is likely to cover only a small percentage of the media target, a group or 'schedule' of titles or programmes is then put together to ensure adequate levels of cover. The level achieved then obviously depends on the budget, as will the frequency, the media planner's job being to achieve the optimum levels of frequency and cover from the schedule at the lowest possible cost. This will initially be a ratecard cost. At some stage in the process of schedule-building – preferably sooner than later – the media buyer will overlay information about the current state of the market, notably whether the ratecard on a given publication or TV station is hard or soft (i.e. capable of downward negotiation). The simplicity of this process is qualified by the central enigma of media planning – that the strategic target rarely corresponds to the media target. This is again where the planner's knowledge of the media, and knowledge of the brand and its advertising and marketing objectives, comes in. Thus, in practice, schedules aren't established solely on the basis of cost-ranking: qualitative judgements also apply. Specifically these involve the planner/buyer's judgement on:

- Whether a given title is particularly likely to be read by buyers of the advertised brand.
- Whether it's a particularly suitable context for the brand. Brands and their advertisements take colour from the company they keep. This is normally called the *environment*.
- Whether it is particularly suitable for the ad or campaign objectives.
- Market conditions: circulation and readership forecasts; soft and hard markets and so on.

If this involves a level of understanding and judgement on the part of the planner – invariably overlain by that of you as the advertiser – so too does the issue of media *size and length*. Longer commercials and bigger ads (press, posters) are naturally in gross media terms more expensive, but at the same time are normally cheaper by the yard, second etc. It follows obviously enough that as space size grows, cover and frequency tend to fall, the compensation lying in the greater impact assumed to be associated with longer and larger ads. This is quite an entertaining subject, and one that marries – or attempts to reconcile – two departments and disciplines within agencies that rarely have much time for one another: media and creative.

Naturally enough the creative view is simple. The bigger the better. Tiny little press ads like 'twenty doubles' and 10 second TV slots aren't really seen as providing much scope for the creative palette, and besides they are rather difficult. Television, it is true, is invariably the most satisfactory medium, but of rather more expansive time-length; and a poster's not really a poster unless it is a forty-eight or, preferably, a ninety-six sheet. Four sheets simply won't do. To be fair this would all be perfectly reasonable if common sense correlated with the consumer, or rather the consumer with common sense. This, however, isn't necessarily so. Leaving aside the issue of cover, response to advertising material is a function of a combination of frequency, size, the message and the manner of expression, and the position of the ad within the medium. Size isn't everything. It tends to compromise other desirable qualities and, in certain circumstances, can be simply counter-productive. Full-page ads and double-page spreads look good on your schedule and on your marketing director's wall. There's a certain completeness about them. Whether the absence of editorial content in the pages on

Table 8.2 A cost-ranking of magazine titles for a food brand

	Unit cost (£)	CPT (£)
Radio Times	14000	76.09
Ideal Home	10000	90.09
BBC Good Food	11500	104.55
Good Housekeeping	14000	106.06
You Magazine	13000	108.33
Woman & Home	8000	112.68
TV Times	8000	119.40
Homes & Gardens	9500	120.25
House & Garden	7500	125.00
Essentials	10000	128.21
She	7000	129.63
Options	4000	133.33
Prima	19000	132.87
Reader's Digest	20000	136.99
Living	5500	152.78
Family Circle	17500	163.55
Telegraph Magazine	9000	163.64
Sunday Express Magazine	9000	166.67
Cosmopolitan	11000	177.42
Me	10000	188.68
Evening Standard Magazine	9500	197.92
House Beautiful	8000	200.00
Vogue	13000	203.12
What's on TV	12000	203.39
Best	21000	207.92
Woman's Journal	4000	210.53
Hello!	10500	214.29
Chat	10000	212.77
Country Homes & Interiors	6000	214.29
Country Living	8000	228.57
Elle	9000	230.77
Sunday Times Magazine	25000	238.10
Observer Magazine	12500	250.00
Independent Magazine	11000	250.00
Bella	30000	256.41
Marie-Claire	6000	260.87
Harpers & Queen	10000	263.16
Company	8000	296.30
Woman's Own	28000	311.11
Take a Break	25000	312.50

Source WCRS

which they appear prevents the reader from noticing them is merely a matter for debate.

Similarly questionable is the issue of *position* within a TV or radio programme, within a given publication, geographically for a poster site. In fact, as ratings are increasingly available for each part of a TV programme – not just the whole – this is fairly easy. Press is a different matter. There is a belief that ads placed towards the front of publications and on the right-hand page are more likely to be noticed than elsewhere; equally that travel ads are best placed in the travel pages etc. Moreover, ratecards frequently reflect these beliefs. For everyone concerned this is a frustrating area. Those concerned with getting the best out of a schedule will undoubtedly concern themselves with position and will usually pay more for it. There is no real way of determining either whether this will be, or has been, money well spent. It is part of the folklore of the industry.

The final issue of media placement is *timing*. This, too, is the subject of entertaining debate. Given that few brands can maintain a continuous advertising presence, the question is a simple one: when should you advertise? As ever, the superficial answer to this is often quite simple and indeed the approach that many agencies and advertisers adopt. The key issue is normally the seasonality of the brand, media normally being placed immediately before, or during, the selling season. The spirits market in many countries is concentrated in the last quarter of each year and most brands put all their spend into this period. This begs the question: is this the right strategy? And what do you do when there's no real selling season? These issues are less straightforward. Synchronising advertising with the sales period passes the common sense test, but assumes that advertising has an immediate and causal effect on sales. Some advertising does do that, but not most. It also ignores the fact that all your competitors are advertising at the same time, so the chance of standing out from the crowd – technically your *share of voice* – in the sector is heavily reduced. It also helps you minimally when, in any case, there's no seasonality to provide a timing focus. Here media planners and their clients often find themselves at sea. There are 'traditional' advertising periods, periods dictated by the availability of client funds, and beliefs like:

1 Everyone goes on holiday in August,
2 so no one watches the television.

Of course, one decision is to make no decision and run a very light weight of activity ('drip' as opposed to 'burst') throughout the year. Depending on the nature of the brand, the nature of the advertising objectives (create awareness, reinforce existing behaviour etc.) and the budget, this may be a sensible option. The other is to take the most pragmatic of approaches and buy at the time when media is cheapest. Media costs vary (by medium) considerably in the course of the year.

The problem here – the general media problem – however remains. Although quantified media research of who – in demographic terms – buys what is increasingly available, most media strategies and schedules are in fact built on an impressive edifice of experience, prejudice, received wisdom and, in some instances, common sense. In the end this isn't terribly satisfactory. It lacks very distinctly the desire to experiment and the need – indeed opportunity – to learn from the past. In the same way as it is impossible to predict the results of advertising generally, so too is it impossible – if anything more so – to predict the results of a given media strategy. What is normally rather more possible is to learn from – sometimes by using different media schedules in different areas – the experience of a particular campaign and particular strategy run in the past. As a practice, though, this is not as common as it should be. Reviews of the impact of advertising are relatively commonplace, as are buying reviews in which the cost of the campaign is compared to ratecard costs. Assessing or trying to assess the performance of a particular media strategy or schedule is unusual; it is worth encouraging your agency to do it.

MEDIA DEPARTMENTS VERSUS MEDIA INDEPENDENTS

All this ultimately raises the question of who should be doing the job – or jobs – described. This is a subject in which advertisers and agencies interest themselves greatly for the simple reason that money – large sums of it – are directly involved. It is also important because it influences the impact of the advertising.

Theoretically the answer to this question is simple: the agency. The key to the effective use of media lies in getting the right fit between the brand's advertising and its medium, and the agency that promotes the brand is in a far better position to achieve that fit than anyone else. So the argument goes. The reality is rather different. Many agency media departments isolate themselves – or are isolated – from the main agency, sometimes geographically. And, as a consequence, the cross-fertilisation of knowledge and ideas that should occur between the people running the account, those doing the ads, and the media planners simply doesn't. At the same time media independents, or the centralised buying units employed by some advertisers, often offer significant bulk discounts based on the very considerable volume of media they buy. In theory, this is certainly an inferior arrangement in so far as it is rare for the centralised media planner – or buyer – to have sufficient time or interest in a particular brand to ensure that the best conjunction between brand and medium is achieved. Against this has to be balanced the cost argument in favour of centralised buying. In many respects it comes down to a quality versus quantity argument, the onus lying on the agency responsible for the creative work to demonstrate that its understanding of the brand and what the advertising is trying to do leads to the more efficient use of media. Conversely, the onus lies on the centralised buyers to demonstrate that lower costs don't lead to a compromise on quality.

It is by no means clear that the media audit procedures increasingly being used by clients contribute very much to either assessment. In principle, the notion of an independent media company policing media-buying is a good one in so far as it incentivises to those responsible to do their jobs and get the best possible deals for their clients. The problem, as ever, lies in the definition of 'best'. In practice, best generally is taken to mean cheapest and, for the reasons already explained, cheapest is by no means always the best way of judging a media strategy.

MEDIA BRIEFING

The drift of all this is really about the importance of regarding media not as an isolated but as an integral part of the marketing and advertising process. Media costs are the largest associated with advertising, and the impact of a campaign depends significantly on how well the media are planned and bought. Media choices depend on what sort of marketing strategies and tactics, and what sort of advertising objectives and creativity, are being used. And therefore the best choices are achieved if the media planning and buying process is an integrated part of that advertising. It follows that, like the briefing of the agency generally, the briefing of media is a continuous and ongoing, informal and formal process. The framework of such a briefing should be as follows:

1 What is the advertising trying to do? Tightly defined objectives concerning themselves with the direct effect of advertising.
2 Whose attitudes, feelings or, possibly, behaviour is it trying to influence? Demographics are the starting, not the finishing, point. We also need to know attitudes towards the brand etc.
3 Where do these people live/where is the brand distributed? Basic regional data.
4 What seasonal influences are there on brand sales/other influences on

campaign timing ? Seasonality of sales is very marked in some product
sectors.

5 What is the creative approach? This should ideally complement the
medium.

6 What is the budget? The starting point for media discussions.

7 What's the competition doing?

Figure 8.3 The media planning cycle

CHECKLIST

1 **Media deserves more time and trouble spent on it than is normally the case.
It is by far the biggest single cost associated with advertising and, although
it is difficult to get it wrong, it is easy to get it not as right as it should be.**

2 **Most countries are now characterised by an extraordinary wealth of media
choice. This makes the advertiser's job of selecting suitable media a
complex business requiring expert advice. Further media fragmentation is
occurring and this will make the job harder. It is the agency's job to keep
abreast of these changes; the advertiser's to make sure this is happening.**

3 **The basic media job involves matching the target audience for the
advertising with the media consumption habits of that target. Getting
better media value involves a closer understanding of the brand and what
the advertising is trying to do; and not simply which media the target
consumes, but also why, how and when.**

4 Two things can help this process: the greater use of qualitative and quantitative research to help put a schedule together; and more careful, empirical assessment of existing schedules.

5 Given the sums of money involved, it is tempting to place media planning and buying with the media independents whose bulk buying promises volume discounts. Given the need to understand the brand, its marketing objectives and its advertising to best place media, this may be a false economy.

6 The real key to getting better media value really lies in the integration of the media planning and buying process with that of the advertising as a whole. As in the creative arena, this begins and ends with better briefing.

9 IT'S A RICH MAN'S WORLD
Producing advertising cost-effectively

Advertising: a source of wealth.

GUSTAVE FLAUBERT
The Dictionary of Received Ideas

*Production values and consumer response · producing TV and print work ·
mark-ups · alternatives to agency production · poachers and gamekeepers ·
controlling costs*

Against all the odds the campaign, that great advertising edifice, is now
gradually taking shape. The planner has crafted an elegant brief.
Apparently by means of Semaphore, Braille or Morse, this has been communicated to the creative department. Some months later a response
tangentially related to the original instructions is presented to you with every
possible obsequy and flourish by account management. Media – always late
on the scene – endorse the use of the television medium so surprisingly used
by the creatives. The proposals are rejected, amended, rejected; the brief
rewritten to accommodate the creative work; the work represented in a
different guise, amended and ultimately approved. The air-date looms, the
point at which you have promised the marketing director the brand will,
finally, be supported. All that remains is to turn the agency's pieces of
cardboard into film and, as a concession to your own prejudice, one, single,
four-sheet poster. The production process has begun.

Production is a hot potato. In the first instance there's little doubt that
production values matter. No one finds a shakily-written, hand-painted sign
advertising 'Bed and Breakfast' hung drunkenly on a farm gate particularly
inviting. The assumption is – rightly or wrongly – that the care, trouble and
attention to detail manifested in the advertisement will be reflected in the
service itself. Presumably in this case bed-bugs, soiled linen and things that
go bump in the night. So, too, is it with more professional forms of advertising. Like it or not, ads are judged as much by the quality with which an
idea is rendered as the quality of the idea itself. The assumption is that the
style is the man. If there is manifest cost-cutting in the production of a TV

commercial, who's to say that that won't appear in the product itself? The anticipation is that it will. The evidence – recent consumer research – is that consumers don't give advertisers the benefit of the doubt. This is in itself sufficiently awkward. It's doubly so now because, generally, production standards are so high. The technological revolution – much of it associated with the computer – provides astonishingly high standards of visual mimicry that the public has come to accept as the norm: animation, magical trans-formations, and the verisimilitude of big-budget science fiction films like *Superman*, *Star Wars* and *Alien* form a bench-mark to which advertisers are obliged to adhere willy-nilly. And it is not even the case that these standards are likely to be particularly admired. The only occasion on which consumers remark about production is when it is below par. Production values – the setting, the casting, the lighting, the acting, the photography – these details matter. Not only is the medium the message, so too is the quality of production. The advertiser is the sponsor of the advertisement. The quality of every aspect of the advertisement reflects on the judgement of the advertiser. It is a symbol – a visible symbol – of the product, intruding into the family living-room.

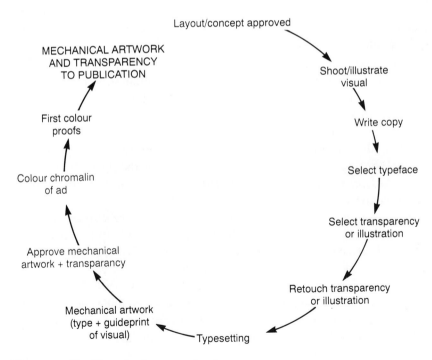

Figure 9.1   The life cycle of a press advertisement

It is not, of course, here that the controversy lies. Neither is it really in how this quality is to be achieved. Most major advertising markets are well served in production terms, and getting the necessary quality is not usually a problem. The issue is rather one of cost. In many respects at face value this is surprising. It is true, of course, that the worldwide market for production is probably in the order of $20 billion, which is quite a lot of money. Still, that's approximately one-tenth of the total world media spend – and 10 per cent of the media spend is the rule-of-thumb figure most advertisers still work to on production. Yet production costs are at least as important an issue as media. This is a paradox, the explanation of which is simple. Advertisers think – sometimes wrongly – that their media buyers provide them with value for money. Advertisers think – occasionally rightly – that their production buyers don't. For years this issue has been a running sore. It has been inflamed once again by recession.

MARK-UPS AND MARK-UPS

Production, like media-buying, has of course traditionally been in the hands of the agency itself. Strictly speaking, though, relatively few agencies actually produce their own ads. The majority have specialised TV and print production units which are buyers of the various production services rather than being producers themselves. In the case of television these people hire directors, production houses, and post-production facilities like dubbing and optical effects. Print production similarly involves the co-ordination by the agency of typesetters, photographers, illustrators, the people who physically bring all these things together into a single piece of art-work, and ultimately the printer. Generally, these are all separate, specialist organisations, although agencies sometimes have financial interests in businesses with which they are, in any case, hand-in-glove. The agency then ensures that this material – termed 'copy' whatever its physical form – is then delivered to the relevant media owner for publication. This seems a sufficiently logical arrangement and in many respects it is. It gives the agency more or less total creative control over something which it originated and for which it is ultimately responsible. It seems sensible that the agency should also co-ordinate the process and be paid for so doing, and the system as it stands also gives the agency a large measure of choice. Different directors, different producers, different typesetters and different photographers are good at different things. It follows that some are going to be better than others at producing given advertisements. A good agency with good production buyers will know that market well, will know who is good at what and will get the best production job done on a particular ad.

Really, that should be the end of the matter. Unfortunately for agencies it is not. Few things – even creative work – excite advertisers more than production costs. Perhaps this is partly less because of what these costs are, but more what they are seen to be: costs. Advertising, of course, isn't a cost. It is an investment – or at least it should be. The same can be said of media. Rightly or wrongly, production isn't so regarded. It is in fact rather like consumers' views of packaging. In other words, something they know they pay for and don't particularly want. There again, with media expenditure, something definite, concrete and objective has been achieved: a schedule delivering a given frequency and coverage of the target. Even better, it can be quantified: if not in its impact, but at least in its general delivery. By comparison, production seems a spurious cost, the return on which is impossible to define. The third issue is unit cost. If gross estimates seem high enough, breakdowns seem less to justify than frequently to astonish. Directors' fees of $20,000 for a 30-second commercial, and $3000 a day for a stills photographer seem rather large. As an advertiser you may compare this with your own pay packet and look askance.

Ultimately though, these matters are peripheral. The real issue lies in

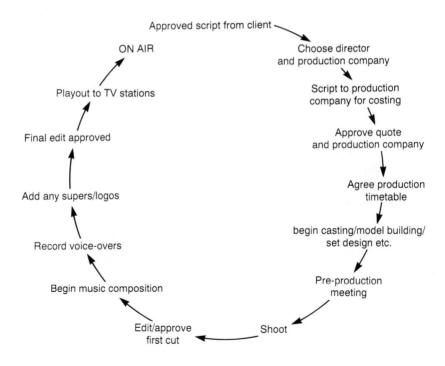

Figure 9.2 The life cycle of a TV commercial

mark-ups. As has been suggested, the job most agencies do in getting ads produced is, in most respects, very good. The buyers usually *do* know their markets and the final results are frequently excellent. This is worth paying for, as is the process of liaison and co-ordination between the various people involved in ad production which most advertisers would find an utterly thankless task. Now, of course, in the same way as agencies traditionally charge a commission on media bought, so too do they generally place one on production. The true cost of media for any campaign is generally a large sum charged by a limited number of media owners, and as a consequence it can be and normally is carefully audited. This means that if an agency has contractually agreed to be paid on a basis of X per cent commission, the commission it takes can be, but on the whole is unlikely to be very far from that figure. On the production side the position is very different. The sums involved are relatively small – particularly in terms of, say, a given press execution – and the number of suppliers involved is large. Close auditing of this process rarely seems worthwhile. The consequence of this is that agencies can make a good deal more than their official commission on production, sometimes to the tune of 100 per cent. This is certainly not an endemic practice but neither is it startlingly rare. Within the marketing – not simply advertising – industry it is a largely open secret. And it irritates the advertising industry's clients.

POACHERS AND GAMEKEEPERS

For many advertisers this matter has now gone beyond anger. True, the gross sums aren't very large, but no one particularly relishes being used as a dupe. And for some companies making tens of commercials, perhaps even hundreds worldwide – the IBMs, Kodaks, Kelloggs and Sonys – the sums, after all, do tot up. These companies aren't in the business of subsidising agencies, production houses and ad make-up units. They are in the business of making profits for their shareholders. It is perhaps not surprising in the current state of the advertising industry that these firms should have found a number of people only too eager to tell them what they wish to hear. The US employs about a third of the world's advertising people and at the last count 10 per cent of them were out of work. And in several other countries the proportion isn't dissimilar. Familiar with the ins and outs of the advertising business, some of these people have turned their knowledge and experience to good use by advising clients on production issues, and setting up companies to do this. These take various forms, from simple propositions like the policing of agency production estimates, to more ambitious organisations that propose to take a hand in production itself. The argument is essentially that bulk-buying by large clients of commodities – and some of these things are commodities – like studio time can lead to significant economies of scale. Their promise to advertisers is simple: cheaper ads with no compromise on quality. This is something that may ultimately be resisted but cannot really in any economic climate be entirely ignored. Nor is it. Major advertisers – minor ones too – presumably keep such approaches as far as possible to themselves and they certainly keep them from their agencies. But what is undoubtedly true is that some leading international advertisers – notably Unilever – have already crossed the Rubicon by significantly divesting their agencies of production responsibilities. And you can bet that as some have already done so, there is a large number of other advertisers busily considering whether this isn't the right way to go.

PRODUCING ADVERTISING COST-EFFECTIVELY

The moral of this story is simple enough. The advertising business, which has for so long failed to put its own house in order, is now being forced, belatedly, to do so by nothing other than market forces. Competition is in the air. The unthinkable has happened. What everyone assumed to be a monopoly actually proves not to be. Naturally enough this all poses the question that many advertisers are already asking: how can I get my advertising most cost-effectively produced? The corollary of this has now become – through circumstances for which agencies have largely themselves to blame – who should produce my advertising? These are questions that are subsidiary to those of strategy, creativity and media, but in situations in which money – and savings – talk, they count.

A point worth reiterating here is the issue of quality. Unless the values of production generally drop – and this seems highly unlikely – the ultimate objective of the production process must be to do the fullest possible justice to the original idea. Production values matter and their absence is noticed by consumers: quality counts. How is that quality is to be obtained? The reality here is that in practice there is little debate. The agency is the originator of the advertising idea and in conceiving it will – normally – have developed concrete, coherent and appropriate ways of executing it. The agency has moral, intellectual and sometimes legal ownership of the idea, and is in these senses best placed to produce it. Agency people also generally work closely with those on the production side and are in the best position to get the right people to do the job and to co-ordinate the business of doing it. And, particularly in the case of an existing campaign, the agency has the experience of producing previous executions, which to an extent guarantees the quality of future work. Advertisers can certainly get their ads produced more cheaply – often more quickly – elsewhere. They are genuinely unlikely to get them produced to a similarly high quality.

If the agency is accepted as the best supplier, the issue then becomes one of cost. Or rather cost-control. There are some costs outside the agency's – or indeed the advertiser's – control, and these are really the unit costs. These often seem expensive, but the extent to which they genuinely are is debatable. The specialists – people like directors, lighting/cameramen and stills photographers – are generally highly talented people who very simply charge what the market will bear. This may mean that they cost a lot to hire. It does not necessarily follow that they are expensive in the sense of being unduly costly. The exception to this rule are film crew costs – dictated in some countries by their unions. There, one may well question quite what the gaffer, best boy and electrician's mate do on the sets; and it may well be that it is the business of television commercial production rather than that of TV itself that is now the last bastion of restrictive practices. This is the main reason why a minute's television commercial often costs the same – very often a great deal more – as an hour's editorial TV.

Of course, within this framework there's almost invariably a certain scope for agency manoeuvre, and a few agencies still take the whole business of supplier costs as an open brief to let the suppliers charge more or less what they like and pass these charges – with interest – on. Given the proven, time-tested inability of these agencies here to prevent the money sticking to their own hands, the best solution is the independent audit. Currently, agencies have no incentive to minimise supplier costs. In fact, the reverse is the case in so far as commission is normally calculated on the gross production cost. A better scheme is to put that aspect of the agency's service on to a fee basis, provide it with incentives on the basis of both cost and quality, and use an independent auditor for the process of so doing. The merit of this is that – unlike the commoner methods of agency renumeration – it means that it's in the agency's own interest to produce good work at a decent price. Generally, it is only in the agency's interest to contrive an expensive price. It is for this sort of role that the poachers turned gamekeepers are admirably suited.

The extent to which other measures should be put into place is much more debatable. A number of agencies have reacted to the production-cost issue by proposing that they should do the job themselves. These notions take various forms, the common idea being that agencies should handle some of the processes they normally farm out. This, they brightly inform their clients, will mean savings for all. In practice it seems as though these ideas are contrary to the lessons of the past and also to common sense. J. Walter Thompson, Collett Dickenson Pearce, Young and Rubicam and Oglivy and Mather have all tried in-house TV production and have all given it up – apparently on the grounds of unprofitability and impracticality. On the matter of common sense, production of any nature needs a combination of investment and expertise: investment in rather expensive machinery like typesetters; expertise by way of people used to doing these things. Agencies breed people interested in the production side, some of whom, suitably trained, would doubtless be very good at it. In the end though, few agencies are prepared to invest, and few have personnel sufficiently experienced to do the job. Savings then, probably yes. But savings at the expense of the quality of the final job.

This means that production is something best left in the hands of the agency itself, but that somehow agencies have to contrive a situation which – at least on the issue of costs – they are, like Caesar's wife, above suspicion. While they are not, you're best advised to use experienced, independent auditors to ensure that the agency is actually providing the value for money it promises, as well as the quality and expertise it genuinely delivers.

If you've taken all this sensible advice, you will now be in the happy position of having a carefully thought-out, creatively exciting campaign that has been produced cost-effectively and will run where your customers will see it. In so doing the second phase of the advertising process is complete.

CHECKLIST

1 Consumers are surprisingly sensitive to the issue of production values. As a consequence it is crucial for advertisers to ensure that all their work is produced to state-of-art standards.

2 Advertising agencies are generally very good at rendering their ideas into finished ads. The problem lies rather in what they charge for so doing. The habit of excessive marking-up means advertisers are now examining these costs more closely than ever before. And in some instances they are going outside the agency to get the ideas produced.

3 The better solution lies in independently auditing agency production costs. There are a number of experienced individuals and companies able to provide such vetting, and agencies increasingly accept this as a necessary process.

4 In-house production by agencies is a natural by-product of this phenomenon. This idea has yet to prove itself, and should be treated with caution.

PART THREE

Our aim is to destroy the view that advertising is a commodity. It is the creation of an elusive spark of originality which can fundamentally enhance a client's business. But in order to create that elusive spark, the relationship between client and agency has to be on a firm footing, embracing both respect and trust.

PETER MEAD
Abbott Mead Vickers

Evaluating the advertising product

'How often have I said to you that when you have eliminated the impossible, whatever remains, *however improbable*, must be the truth?'

SIR ARTHUR CONAN DOYLE
The Sign of Four

Pressures to evaluate advertising · difficulties of doing so · four awkward questions · the irrelevance of sales data · the misleading nature of advertising tracking · the dangers of gossip · the temptation to despair · the holistic approach · how to do it · the brand monitor · case for the independent auditor

As this book is about how to produce more effective advertising, so far we've been looking at ways in which the various processes involved in producing a campaign can be honed. In so doing all sorts of approaches have been considered from which, in theory, the best possible advertising can be obtained. Ultimately, however, this is theory because it concerns itself with contriving material that *should* work better, not that necessarily will. Given that every effort has been made in the selection of the agency, its briefing, the development of targeting, the message and creative work, the evolution of an appropriate media strategy and even some judicious creative development research, you can now do nothing more than launch the frail barque of advertising and see if it actually works. The only snag in this, of course, is that while no advertising manager who wishes to keep the job has much choice other than to run at least some sort of material, like Lord Leverhuime he or she may indeed then find that having aired the campaign, it is very difficult to decide which half of it really *does* work.

The desirability of so doing goes without saying, recession merely adding further force to the need for accountability long sought by advertisers themselves, yet not always embraced with as much enthusiasm by agencies as might be expected. Advertising for all firms is an investment in the usual sense of a sum expended on which a return is expected; for most it represents more than half of total promotional costs; and for a number a significant sum straight off the bottom line. Shareholders will accordingly very reasonably ask whether this is money well spent; so too will a company's internal auditors; so too will those in management disciplines other than marketing with their own budgets to foster; so above all will marketers themselves – particularly those who believe in the empirical approach to advertising. More than ever before the advertising business is 'justifiably expected to produce convincing evidence in its own defence'; it is under increasing pressure to do so, and it is in its own interests to demonstrate how, where, why and when its product does or doesn't work. The worldwide spend on advertising in 1991 was $210 billion. This is the equivalent of the combined GNP of Belgium, Portugal, Denmark and Ireland. Did it work?

THE HILL DIFFICULTY

The question then isn't so very reasonable. It is a misfortune shared by those who work in marketing as well as the wider business world that the answer still seems to remain so elusive. From virtually everyone's point of view it would be highly attractive to say that as a consequence of $5 million advertising investment, the return took the form of sales increased to an extent more than sufficient to cover the cost – indeed preferably by a factor of ten. Yet in the vast majority of cases no such simple equation can exist. If it is true that advertising works, it is quite simply very difficult to tell if particular campaigns or executions work.

This is partly because the way in which advertising generally works is indirect. Of course, there's not, in the first instance, general agreement on how advertising works at all, various more or less imaginative ideas on the mechanism of the advertising process circulating from time to time. Still, it is true that most agencies tacitly – often it seems unconsciously – accept the broadly traditional view that advertising works in a manner summarised by the acronym AIDA: it creates an **A**wareness of brands and stimulates **I**nterest in them; this in turn leads to consumer **D**esire and ultimately **A**ction.

Obviously there are various weaknesses in this sort of model. To start with, the pleasingly logical domino effect it proposes – awareness leading to interest to desire etc. – is patently divorced from the ramshackle and inconsequential way in which most of our minds work, and generally how we go about choosing brands. Equally, it somehow implies that all ads work in the same way, something which is almost certainly untrue; and that advertising has a quite powerful effect on people, a fact that many – including consumers themselves – dispute. Yet what is clear is that – if you believe advertising *does* work – it must work more or less along the lines proposed, even if by no means exactly and by no means invariably in this way. At its

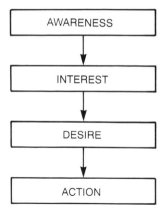

Figure 10.1 AIDA

simplest, advertising reminds people of the existence of brands, portrays them in a flattering light and thereby encourages consumers to buy. If this broad model is accepted, it follows that the process is far from simple cause and immediate, direct effect; far more one in which advertising is fairly tenuously and indirectly related to the human action that is its ultimate aim, much distanced as it is in both time and place from the action it is supposed to predicate. Moreover, if advertising is a peripheral influence on behaviour, it is not the only peripheral influence but one of a number. At its most basic level, whether or not a consumer buys a brand depends on the appeal of the product, the brand's availability and its price. Consumers are also obviously influenced to a lesser or greater extent by a myriad of other factors ranging from price promotions to the colour of the pack and whether or not Aunt May's coming to tea today. The consequence of this is, of course, that while some sort of sales effect is the only ultimate justification for advertising investment in a brand, confidently and quantifiably to associate the one with the other is difficult.

If this is partly because of the peripheral *way* in which advertising works, it is also a consequence of the period of time over which it works, and the fact that its job is more often than not to help maintain an existing position rather than to increase volume and share.

The idea that advertising has medium to long-term effects, as well as shorter ones, is largely familiar. Advertising in certain circumstances can achieve a short-term quantifiable impact, sometimes on sales and often on what are usefully called 'surrogate' measures such as advertising awareness and imagery. Equally it can work over longer periods in establishing and reinforcing brand identity in a way which appears to support price premiums, encourage consumer loyalty, provide barriers to competitive entry and all sorts of other desiderata. Appreciating these points, a number of imaginative and prescient companies in the UK persisted in advertising during the Second World War, when their products were minimally available, so as to maintain their cachet with the public – notably Cadbury's the chocolate people and Van den Berghs (Stork margarine). More recently, a compelling case (by the advertising agency Boase Massimi Pollitt/Doyle Dane Bernbach) has been made for the way in which the very long-running British campaign for PG Tips tea, featuring chimpanzees, has enabled the brand to minimise the impact of competitive new product development, fight off the challenge of shops' own-label tea, and sustain significant margins in a market threatened by commoditisation. These 'longer and broader' effects – a new category in the effectiveness awards run by Britain's Institute of Practitioners in Advertising – are doubtless highly desirable. Yet their existence manifestly complicates the issue of assessing the impact of advertising. In acknowledging that advertising works over considerable periods of time – and in manners not invariably associated with simple, incremental sales effects – it forces us to measure advertising over longer periods and in more broadly-based ways. It would be jolly useful to know within a six-month period whether the advertising has worked, whether further investment is justified and, if so, how much. Generally this is impossible.

The other problem in seeking an advertising effect is that although there is normally no justification in advertising that doesn't have a (short or long-term) impact on sales, that effect will by no means invariably be an upward one. Of course, in growing markets, merely to maintain volume is to lose share and ultimately to dilute brand equity, let alone failing to grasp a sales opportunity. Yet, as the advertising researcher Colin Macdonald has pointed out in a recent paper on monitoring advertising performance, many consumer markets are for practical purposes mature. This means that they already appeal to consumers as much as they ever will and that their growth, at least in volume terms, is either static or in slow decline. Now, in these circumstances, the purpose of some marketing and most advertising activity may very reasonably be to *maintain* existing volumes or share against competitive encroachment, rather than to increase them. Brands in this position have already established themselves and in certain respects have nowhere else to go but down. For them the maintenance of the existing sales position may well be the only realistic aim. Now, if this is the case, advertising may well play a part in achieving the objective, but of course there will be no easily quantifiable growth in sales to 'justify' an advertising investment. This supportive function of advertising – it fits the 'reinforcement' box in advertising strategy – is in fact probably more common than is normally acknowledged. Simon Broadbent of Leo Burnett has likened this situation to the engine powering an aeroplane in level flight. When the engine is switched off the plane plummets, Broadbent describing some entertaining case histories demonstrating this effect. As advertising does indeed, in some cases appear to work in this way, it is a little naïve always to be looking for the magical sales blip . . .

Advertising, then, is difficult to measure because it affects human action indirectly, because it is one of a number of things so doing, because it affects it over longer as well as shorter periods, and because its effect, as well as its entirely legitimate objective, may be to sustain as much as increase sales.

HOW NOT TO MEASURE ADVERTISING

Now although it is probably fair to say that this thinking is notionally accepted by the marketing community, it remains the case that its implications aren't always manifested when it comes to the ways in which advertising is assessed. This means that once the campaign is up and running, as ad manager you are likely to have to fend off four awkward and ultimately rather misleading questions.

The first of these questions is almost invariably: *How are sales*? This at least is an easy one for, as has been suggested, this is relatively rarely a reasonable way in which to evaluate advertising, because:

- advertising doesn't normally impact directly on sales;
- its objective may be to help maintain rather than increase sales;
- sales may well rise (or fall) at the same time as an advertising campaign for reasons other than the advertising's impact;
- much advertising has and is intended to have medium rather than short-term impact. It will therefore have a cumulative effect on 'sales'.

This means that, generally, this is an unhelpful question to ask.

(A question that offers a slightly more useful variation in certain circumstances is: *How is rate of sale*? FMCG is the best-documented and best-researched trade sector in which advertising is often the biggest variable in the marketing mix. Services such as Nielsen offer reasonably accurate rate-of-sale (ROS) data – supermarkets in the US are now themselves offering similar services – and this quite often displays sensitivity to advertising. The argument then is normally that rises and falls of ROS are coincident with advertising and therefore may be attributed to it. These tend to be good rather than impregnable cases and if some sort of ROS effect is a marketing objective, then a control area in which advertising isn't being used is a good idea. The other point to remember is that ROS effects, while pleasing for all concerned, are not likely to be the *only* effects of the advertising. This is important because the revenue derived from increased rate-of-sale rarely in itself pays for the advertising activity.)

Slightly more helpful is question two – *How is share?* The point of share figures is of course that they reflect individual brand performance in the context only of the immediate sector competition – say, other condoms. They therefore eliminate broader social and economic effects, making those unique to your sector more apparent. If you've just ended a major campaign and sales are considerably down, if the sector as a whole is falling and you've nevertheless grown your share, the advertising may well have 'worked'. However, like sales figures, share still clearly reflects the impact of a several of variables, only one of which is advertising.

To be fair, most advertisers are entirely aware that sales and share are a beguiling but ultimately not very accurate guide to whether or not their advertising is working. Many larger advertisers will therefore ask the third key question: *How is the campaign tracking?*

Quite how commonplace this form of evaluation of advertising is on a worldwide basis it is difficult to say, but it's probably true that it is the usual method of measuring campaigns of any significance – say those on which $2 million or more is being spent. They are quantitative studies which involve fairly large numbers – hundreds – of interviews with consumers, conducted before, after, and sometimes during the advertising campaign. Superficially, this sort of thing is a far better way of measuring whether and how well the advertising is working because it appears to be measuring what the advertising is seeking to do directly – raising brand awareness, for example – rather than ultimately: raising or at least affecting sales. In this way it seems to be a method of measuring the sort of defined objectives for advertising discussed earlier. Usually, such studies concern themselves with three basic areas:

- whether people have noticed the advertising;
- what they think the advertising is trying to get across;
- what they think and feel about the advertised brand.

These measures splendidly pass the common-sense test without necessarily being quite as useful as might at first appear. To take them in turn.

1 Advertising awareness is a very useful measure of advertising awareness but not necessarily much else. In poorly-branded advertising, raising *advertising* awareness may not significantly affect *brand* awareness. And

even if it does, raising brand awareness won't necessarily affect sales. The fact that your ads have been noticed by large numbers of C2Ds is not in itself proof of success, unless that was an objective of the advertising.

2 It is important – probably – that advertising communicates a 'message', but asking consumers to verbalise that communication isn't necessarily a good way of ensuring that this is happening. Much advertising – particularly TV advertising – is relatively complex and concerns itself as much with communicating a 'personality' or 'image' as specific facts. Personalities can't be easily verbalised and rarely are by C2Ds. Equally it is possible to get some sort of message out of an ad without necessarily being consciously aware of this. This means that the monitor doesn't necessarily monitor whether the advertising message is getting home.

3 Similarly, brand image banks have significant limitations. The very fact that they appear as an essential part of most monitors somehow implies a causal relationship between advertising and brand imagery. This is not quite so. Imagery is obviously a function of a large number of factors, of which advertising is only one. Brand image banks measure brand image. They don't measure the contribution made by advertising to image – although they may help such an evaluation over time.

This means that measures of this sort – communication, awareness, imagery – can ultimately be misleading. They can rightly be called 'surrogate' measures because they are not in themselves accurate gauges of how – or if – the advertising is working, which is a more complicated process than monitors can normally embrace. They are things that *can* be quite easily and cost-effectively measured, and they may well be related to indicators that show whether the advertising works, but they are not in themselves those indicators.

This is one difficulty with the tracking study method and unfortunately not the only one. As Winston Fletcher, a past president of Britain's Institute of Practitioners in Advertising, has pointed out, although advertisers and their agencies tend to talk and think of many of their brands as 'mass-market', this is really true only of utilities like gas, electricity and the telephone. Few brands that we think of as 'mass-market' are bought by more than – say – 15 per cent of the population in the course of a year. And as a third of users of any brand normally account for 70–80 per cent of consumption, that means that even 'mass-market' really comprises no more than 5 per cent of the population. This in turn suggests that, with the sort of sample size normally associated with brand monitors, research agencies are unlikely to be able to recruit at a reasonable cost significant numbers of people who really *do* matter to the brand and who may well be the primary target for the advertising: existing users. Research quotas tend to embrace everyone in the product sector, insufficiently the 5 per cent specifically interested in a given brand.

The final problem is that most monitors are designed to measure advertising – or advertising surrogate measures – rather than specific sorts of advertising. As has been remarked in an earlier chapter, advertising is a generic term covering a number of activities. Within the general area of brand-building activity, a distinction between advertising that announces, challenges, reinforces or entertains can usefully be drawn. Not unreasonably, if the advertising is designed to do one of these particular things, it should be evaluated as to whether it is in fact so doing, rather than by some other criteria. The problem here lies in the tendency for advertising monitors to be designed for the general purposes of evaluating advertising rather than the specific purpose of helping to measure a particular campaign or run for a particular brand, at a particular time. For clearly – without going into the details of questionnaire design – a campaign intended to 'inform' has to be measured in a different way to one intended to 'entertain'. Currently, circumstances militate against this. Syndicated studies – either between or within companies – by their very nature permit little leeway in terms of design to accommodate the peculiarities of advertising for each particular brand.

This all means that tracking studies are a useful and quite cost-effective way of providing pointers as to the way in which brand, advertising and the consumer interact. What they are *not* is what they sometimes purport or are imagined to be: monitors of whether or not the advertising works.

The fourth issue you're likely to have to deal with is the anecdotal assessment of advertising. This involves the question: *What does everyone else think?* Even if the advertising isn't tried by sales or tried by tracking, there is little advertising of any shape or size that will escape this sort of inquisition. In certain respects there's not much to be done about this because advertising is an intrinsically public medium and you don't really need to ask the question: you'll have comments foisted on you whether you like it or not by everyone from the chairman to the landlord of the local pub. The problem with this sort of information is that it is individuals with minds very much their own who remain unaffected by this sort of bombardment – be it negative or positive – and that this sort of comment is, ultimately, irrelevant. Of course, most advertising is expected and sometimes intended to have a subsidiary positive effect on company staff and sales-force; and it is generally desirable that it doesn't have a negative one. Nevertheless, in most cases this is very much a subsidiary objective. The primary one is – of course – to affect the sentiments of the people buying the brand, rather than those making or retailing it. The problem lies in the fact that the very proximity of the secondary target gives it a far louder voice than its far more important, yet distant, cousin. This can be a real issue for marketers running major campaigns, for – as has been suggested before – what pleases the public and helps sell the brand isn't invariably the same thing as pleases an internal audience; and it may in certain circumstances be rather the reverse.

HOW TO MEASURE ADVERTISING

So where does this get you? The argument so far is that evaluating an advertising investment is a highly desirable process; that it's a crucial one if you believe in the empirical approach to advertising; that for a number of reasons it is equally a difficult one; and that the normal questions asked and the usual way of measuring campaigns contribute only in a rather limited way to doing so. In these circumstances you may well feel that all further efforts are pointless, and that the advertising and its merits should stay happily within the realms it has so long inhabited as a black art practised by agencies, requiring an act of faith on the part of the advertiser by way of assessing the advertising, rather than anything more objective. And even in 1993 there are some agencies which still adopt something approaching this stance. Ultimately though, this won't do. Some advertising certainly does work and can be shown to work, and it is to the benefit of agencies, advertisers and marketers generally to ensure that this fact gets about. Agencies as the decade progresses are going to have to do better than 'Trust us. This will work.'

Doing so – at least on major campaigns – requires the adoption of what could be called a holistic approach. This simply means that to evaluate advertising adequately, efforts have to be made to set such activity in the larger, longer and broader context of marketing activities as a whole, thereby relating it to the other factors that affect the standing of a brand, and as far as possible isolating the impact of advertising. You have to act on Sherlock Holmes's principle, that, having 'eliminated the impossible, what-ever remains, *however improbable*, must be the truth'.

This is not a simple or single-minded approach which at a stroke installs some technique or device that at the turn of a handle or the press of a button answers the question: Is the advertising working? Neither is it new. Rather, it is an approach which acknowledges the multifarious influences on buyer behaviour, and makes serious, continuous and long-term efforts to under-stand the nature and weight of each. Its challenge is essentially organisa-tional and interpretative. It requires the co-ordination and consolidation of data from all sorts of sources to establish a coherent picture of the brand and what's happening to it, ultimately in some circumstances econometric models of brand behaviour. And it also needs someone to interpret that information.

The principle is both simple and familiar. As has been suggested above, one of the problems central to advertising evaluation is that the relationship between advertising and buyer behaviour is far from the simple, causal one that would in certain respects be so convenient. Rather, this behaviour is a consequence of a number of factors. Some are important, some less so, and they vary with product sectors, brand, time of year, sun-spot activity etc. The brand audit suggested at the beginning of the book is an attempt to enumerate and analyse what these factors, on any given brand in the first instance, are. The 'holistic' approach to advertising evaluation takes this process a step further by looking at the dynamics of these factors, trying to discover how they affect the brand over a period of time.

The core factors common to every brand that need to be tracked are as follows.

The product

This is often rather less of a fixed quantity than might be supposed. Even where a brand and its packaging remain unchanged for years, many companies pursue a policy of evolutionary and unheralded product development. More obviously, companies are constantly introducing new lines and product variations. These things may influence consumer sentiment and behaviour.

The price

This is the single most important influence in purchasing behaviour in many markets, yet a factor occasionally underestimated by agencies in their concern with image. The key to price tracking is to appreciate, and as far as possible monitor, the level of discounting that occurs in certain markets at certain times. The 'trade' in each sector may be coy about revealing over the phone actual rather than recommended retail prices, but this information can normally be collected on an anecdotal basis. It is also worth remarking on the quite large variations in the prices of branded goods both regionally and within different outlets in the same town. These points complicate what might at first seem a simple issue.

Distribution

The availability of a product is obviously a crucial marketing issue and, if anything, is becoming even more important as retailers – particularly of groceries – become daily more sophisticated in measuring what sells and how quickly it sells. The most important for most brands is, of course, volume of distribution, but as the concept of value gradually overtakes that of cost, the quality of distribution is increasingly important.

Competitive activity

For obvious reasons the competitor's product, price, distribution – and promotional activity – is, in certain respects as important as a brand's own.

Communication

As Chapter 1 suggests, the point here from the perspective of tracking is the importance of keeping an eye on *all* communication activity, rather than advertising as the most glamorous, time-consuming and expensive. The two key points are obviously the nature of the activity and its weight.

Sales

Perhaps the most surprising of many things advertising agencies find surprising about their clients is their relative ignorance of this quite important factor. The ultimate aim is, of course, to know how much is sold to whom, where and at what price, and also how things are changing. And to have this information soon after the event.

Any other business

This includes any other factors that might have affected awareness, imagery or sales – for instance negative or positive PR coverage. Red wine sales in the US are said to have risen 40 per cent in the weeks after a TV documentary associated drinking red wine with lower rates of heart disease.

WAYS AND MEANS

So all you have to do to see if the advertising is working is to collect this data, on a regular basis, to correlate it, and periodically to review it. Collecting the data is the first issue.

To look at the basic categories in turn, marketing departments will naturally be aware of major *product* developments, but are sometimes less aware than they should be of gradual evolution. This can significantly affect consumer behaviour. On *price,* syndicated services like Nielsen provide reliable data in the grocery markets. In other markets the company sales-force is often an invaluable source of anecdotal evidence. With *distribution*, the problem is less the quantitative side than the qualitative. Some sort of quality segmentation of distribution needs to be provided by the quantitative syndicates, but outside FMCG markets this is exceptional. Again, the sales-force is a source of information. An overview of what *competing brands* are up to should be acquired as a matter of course as you are looking at your own brand's position. *Sales data* are now almost invariably available. It is more a question of getting hold of it in usable, summary form.

Communication should be positioned very clearly as part of the advertising agency's brief. Agencies have to hand the resources to track the nature and weight of competitive advertising activity, and on major brands can usually be expected to produce professional reviews. As the fashion is increasingly for agencies to offer a total communication service, they should show themselves competent in this field by tracking all communication activity, not simply advertising. As communication specialists they are in the best position to assess the merit of these activities. It is here that a version of the advertising monitor can be of considerable value. This broadens the conventional ad tracking study into a *communication* monitor which looks at all communication activity about a brand, rather than just the advertising. Despite their limitations, these pieces of research can and do give worthwhile insights into the communication equation. So too can their qualitative equivalents. Examining how people react to the finished commercial once it has been on air for some time can give some insights into how and why it is (or isn't) working. This is especially the case if it is in used in conjunction with other data. All this data can be summarised in the sort of table shown opposite.

The problem then lies in the correlation and interpretation of these data, the process of advertising evaluation at this stage becoming less of a science and more of an art, more an area where experience and expertise are at a premium. The basic process is simple enough, the analyst's job being, as far as possible, to explain general movements in the market, and in particular volume and share changes in the company's own brands, isolating one or two of the variables in the marketing mix that seem to be primarily responsible for changes. Given that the job involves comparing like with unlike – advertising versus distribution effects, competitive price promotion versus the launch of a new line – a degree of experience and proven talent is

	Product	Price	Distribution	Communication	Competition	Sales
Period 1	STATIC	STATIC	Your brand is taken on by a major retailer	Your sponsorship of the Olympics is announced	Brand X launches its new ad campaign	Slight share growth but volume loss
Period 2	You launch a minor variant on regional test	STATIC	STATIC	STATIC	Brand Y undergoes a management buy-out	STATIC
Period 3	STATIC	Drop due to sales promotion	STATIC	You launch your new ad campaign	Brand Z relaunches	The market is recovering but your share's only static
Period 4	The variant is withdrawn following a barrage of consumer complaints	STATIC	Your brand is dropped by a major retailer	The campaign's second burst begins	STATIC	Volume and share fall

Figure 10.2 Marketing snakes and ladders

obviously essential if sense is going to be made of the information.

This fact – among others – perhaps begs a final question as to who should be responsible for establishing a series of processes that may be called, with some accuracy, a *brand monitor*. There are two obvious candidates: the company's own marketing department and its advertising agency. Both, in fact, in a sense disqualify themselves: the marketers because generally they aren't advertising specialists; the agency because it isn't in its own interests to be impartial about its own advertising. This is to exaggerate and, between them, the two will normally do a good job. The alternative is to use an external auditor to lead the process. Although far from common practice, the increasing pressure to understand, analyse and account for marketing and advertising expenditure may justify such an approach in larger firms.

With such an audit in place – an audit at the heart of the empirical approach to advertising – the advertising cycle is now approaching completion. Or so it seems.

CASE HISTORY 4
Screwing up heroin – evaluating the anti-drugs campaign

Drug abuse is a serious social problem endemic in major western cities. It's tackled by the authorities in various ways with varying degrees of enthusiasm and success, the British in the mid-1980s taking the unprecedented step of using advertising to help stem what was then quite fast-rising abuse. This was a bold step because whereas advertising is an established tool for urging people to buy things, it was untried and untested as a way of trying to *prevent* people doing something, let alone preventing them taking drugs. There was also the belief in some quarters that advertising could be counter-productive: it would publicise the issue, draw attention to and glamorise the whole business.

The objectives of the campaign were:

- to raise *awareness* of drug abuse as a major social issue;
- to *inform* those at risk (mainly youngsters) of some of the specific effects and dangers of drugs, and particularly heroin;
- to change *attitudes* towards heroin, discouraging the more favourable;
- in *behavioural* terms to discourage trial.

Developed by the Yellowhammer agency under the auspices of what was then the Department of Health and Social Security, the campaign took a multi-media approach (TV, radio, posters and press). Themed 'Heroin Screws You Up', it focused on the degradation of drug-taking, and some of the specific mental, physiological and psychological effects of heroin abuse.

The problems in assessing its effects were as follows:

- The campaign was a national one, with no control areas in which attitudes and behaviour in the absence of advertising could be assessed.
- The campaign wasn't the only media variable in the 'market', editorial coverage of the issue being very substantial.
- Whereas changes in understanding and attitudes can be measured with some accuracy, behavioural issues are far more difficult. At least at the moment, Nielsen doesn't cover the illicit drugs market.
- Similarly, other 'marketing' variables such as distribution and price were, for obvious reasons, difficult or impossible to measure.

In these unusually awkward circumstances, it was accepted that a large quantitative survey of the target was the best way of assessing the campaign. This project – conducted by Research Business Limited – measured attitudes, understanding and claimed behaviour, in the context of awareness of both advertising and more general editorial media activity.

Two years into the campaign – and with a relatively modest advertising spend of £4 million – the results were as follows.

1 Awareness

Ninety-six per cent of the target claimed to be aware of the advertising against heroin abuse, the campaign supplanting media editorial as a source of information about the issue. Recognition of the advertising was 89 per cent for a TV commercial, 86 per cent for a print ad, 73 per cent a poster, 58 per cent a radio commercial. This was described by the research agency as 'very high for an advertising campaign, denoting a very memorable campaign'.

2 Attitudes and beliefs

A number of areas of belief and attitude showed significant and positive changes. The most important were:

- increased awareness of the symptoms/health consequences of heroin usage (particularly those featured in the advertising campaign);
- decreased perception of any benefits from heroin usage;
- increased specificity to health problems associated with heroin;
- decreased beliefs that taking heroin via sniffing or smoking is less addictive;
- increased belief in death as an inevitable consequence of heroin usage;
- decreased likelihood of accepting an offer of heroin made by a friend;
- more confident specific reasons given in support of refusal.

3 Behaviour

This was simultaneously the most important issue and the most difficult to measure. The table overleaf shows the percentages of the sample *claiming* they would definitely not try, or be very unlikely to try, heroin if offered by a friend. This shows encouraging falls in the likelihood of rejection, particularly among those closer to the drug world and more at risk.

As is often the case, it is not possible here to make a definitive assessment of the impact of the advertising, and specifically the extent to which it met its objectives – especially as the monitor was the only real way of measuring the campaign. What is reasonable, however, is to draw together evidence which collectively points to a particular conclusion. The facts are that over a given period, awareness of the heroin issue increased substantially, the target's understanding and attitudes towards heroin changed significantly, and behaviour if offered the drug hypothetically improved. These changes were coincident with advertising – which the target recalled very well – which focused on these specifics; and they were less clearly associated with general

	Stage I No %	Very unlikely %	Stage II No %	Very unlikely %	Stage III No %	Very unlikely %	Stage IV No %	Very unlikely %	Stage V No %	Very unlikely %
Total sample	83	11	93	4	94	4	93	3	93	4
Tried any drug	75	13	88	6	94	3	83	3	83	7
known heroin/cocaine user/trier	77	12	90	6	94	4	92	2	92	4
Been offered any drug	81	11	92	4	93	4	88	6	88	5
Known someone using drug	80	12	89	6	94	4	90	5	91	4
Agree using heroin once harmless	72	17	89	7	93	6	86	7	85	9
Agree trying any drug will do you harm	90	7	95	3	94	3	97	1	96	3
No contact with drug	87	9	96	3	95	3	95	2	95	4

Source RBL

media coverage. Thus, as the research company concluded, 'the high salience of the advertising campaign and the close relationship of some of the effects to issues featured in the campaign suggests that advertising may have played a major part in the effects reported over the five research stages'.

In the absence of information on the issues of distribution, price and actual 'sales' or usage, this is probably as far as it is reasonable to go, even though Yellowhammer would have substituted 'may have' for 'probably did'.

CHECKLIST

1 Accurately evaluating advertising investment is an increasingly desirable and desired part of the advertising process, central to an empirical approach to the advertising process. It is also quite difficult.

2 This is partly because advertising has an indirect effect on a brand's stature, ultimately its sales; partly because it is one of a number of other things which also directly and indirectly affect the brand; partly because it has long as well as short-term effects.

3 The usual ways of measuring whether advertising is working involve looking at sales and share data, seeing if the campaign is tracking well, and hearing from all and sundry as to whether or not it is any good. None of these is very helpful.

4 The best way of measuring major advertising campaigns is the holistic approach. This attempts to set advertising in the broader context of a brand's total marketing activity and environment, in so doing isolating particular advertising effects.

5 It may be helpful to employ an external advertising auditor to conduct this analysis.

11 STREETS FLOODED.
PLEASE ADVISE
How to advertise abroad

On a summer vacation trip Benchley arrived in Venice and immediately wired a
friend: 'STREETS FLOODED. PLEASE ADVISE'

R. E. BRENNAN
Algonquin Wits

*Into the wild blue yonder · company organisation and culture · the cost
argument · slaughtering lambs · similarities and differences between home
and local markets · strategic issues · creative ones · the media problem ·
advertising evaluation · how to advertise abroad*

It is at this stage in the advertising process – where evidence is appearing that
the ads may actually be working – that you may very reasonably heave a
great sigh of relief and rush off on holiday to Phuket, Aspen, New Delhi or
Timbuktu. You've worked immensely hard at drawing the tooth of a campaign from the agency, and you deserve a rest. This is when the board hands
down the decision to take the campaign abroad, and it is at this point for
many advertisers that their troubles really start.

It is inevitable as the world becomes a smaller place that companies will
increasingly seek to distribute and sell their brands outside their national
market-places. As a phenomenon this really began with the growth of
multinational companies in the 1960s, when these operations, in pursuit of
greater turnover and profit – and in defence against other companies
pursuing similar policies – sought to expand abroad. At the same time it was
claimed that the moves were a response to consumer needs. In the good old
days when countries operated economically, socially and culturally in splendid isolation, consumer needs naturally differed to an extent. The growth of
communications (postal, telegraph, radio, TV), of transport (sea, air) and of
mass-market travel equally inevitably brought cross-fertilisation and the
drawing together of consumer needs; also human desires – generally quite
another thing. It was the role – the opportunity – of multinationals to fulfil,
perhaps create those needs by taking essentials like Guinness, Kellogg's

corn flakes, Johnnie Walker whisky and Sony Walkmans into the great, white, open spaces on the world map – even into the kitchen and living-room of Ernest Dichter's famous new World Consumer. Thus, the advent of the single European market, the opening up of the Eastern bloc, and signs of certain relaxations in the regime in China are merely hastening a worldwide assault on trade barriers which was already occurring. And at the same time, the whole business is merely something which replicates on a larger scale the transition in many countries during the last century from regional to national economies and, as a consequence, regional to national brands. Much as a company in the Düsseldorf of 1892 began to seek customers in Bonn, so too now will successful Italian, Spanish and Dutch brands seek sales throughout the EC, and those in Australia throughout the Pacific Rim. More practically this all means that ever increasingly it is the marketer's job to rise to the challenge of marketing and advertising their goods abroad.

And challenge it is because advertising abroad is difficult. That's not, of course, to imply that advertising at home is easy. As the drift of this book has suggested, the advertising business sets a multitude of traps for the unwary, all ultimately stemming from the considerable value in actually advertising, coupled with the equally considerable difficulties in getting what *appears* to be good advertising; and ensuring that it actually is so. Advertising in any circumstances is difficult. It is simply that advertising in foreign markets is doubly – perhaps triply – so. This is essentially a consequence of the fact that, like the past, abroad is another country: they do things differently there. As a rule:

- they speak another language;
- they have different values;
- they have different trade structures;
- they have different media arrangements;
- they have different advertising legislation;
- they have different expectations from advertising;
- they have different forms of competition;
- they have different pricing structures;
- they are over there.

These things pose difficulties because each is something that in normal circumstances would have some sort of impact on the advertising produced for a brand. It follows that the key to such advertising lies in what can be the very time-consuming process of getting to understand all the major differences between the home and foreign market and, crucially, deciding which impact upon the advertising and in what ways. If this seems complicated, it is – quite. The only good news is that for many marketing people and their agencies the problems are increasingly focusing on the issue of whether or not the home campaign can effectively be run abroad.

CULTURE AND ANARCHY

The starting-point then is the home market and in fact not even the advertising, for it is *company culture*, rather than reason, procedure and logic that first shapes the nature of advertising run abroad. It is often, of course, inaccurate to grace the way in which firms go about their business as a philosophy, but many organisations do in fact have some sort of amalgam of principle, precept and practice – sometimes written down on a piece of paper. These things undoubtedly manifest themselves in the matter of advertising, and naturally enough on how to advertise abroad. In this particular context, there are perhaps three sorts of company that are usefully definable:

- those with centralised marketing philosophies;
- those with decentralised philosophies;
- and those between the two extremes.

What these definitions mean in reality is pretty obvious. The former give local operating companies little freedom in their marketing operations, imposing brand strategy and much of marketing activity – including advertising – on the local companies from above. Their counterparts, the decentralisers, whatever they do in practice, at least speak of giving local operators the maximum autonomy and flexibility. For instance, in Rein Rijkens' *European Advertising Strategies*. Helmut Mancher, chairman and CEO of Nestlé, is quoted as declaring:

We will never erode the responsibilities of our national managers . . . yes, there is an important staff function, recommending strategies for a number of our products on a worldwide basis, but the final decision will always take place at national level.

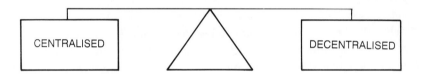

Figure 11.1 Autocracy vs. autonomy

Most companies fall between the two ends of the balance shown in Figure 1.11.

Needless to say, these corporate facts of life have much bearing on what is done about the advertising. If final decisions are taken at national level, foisting a highly successful Spanish campaign on Portugal, France and Italy is likely to prove an uphill struggle. Conversely, if marketing is a centralised process, running thirteen different campaigns in thirteen different countries is unlikely, as a project, to be well received by head office – however different those thirteen countries may be.

The other general point to bear in mind is *company organisation*. Contrary, perhaps, to popular belief, cultures and philosophies are normally developed to justify company organisation rather than vice versa. But, whichever came first, both do matter. The fact is that 'local operating companies' come in a number of different guises. They range from those concerned with little more than the distribution of the brand and on a very tight rein from head office; to something far more autonomous, producing as well as distributing the brand, enjoying a fair degree of local control and, sometimes, a level of local ownership. Again, these things matter. If the arrangement is the former, the local operator may well see eye-to-eye with head office on the question of a centrally-run, centrally-funded advertising campaign. Semi-autonomous operators are in a rather different position. They may well have once been independent companies, and can have established relationships with local ad agencies. This is a different game, and in fact one that is not really within the scope of this chapter. There the answer to the question 'How do you best advertise abroad?' is 'Let them get on with it and hope for the best'.

Issues arise when – as in the majority of cases – the company culture and organisation falls between the two extremes and, with a campaign that is apparently successful safely in the bag, the marketing director passes on the board's directive to you to take it to New Zealand, Czechoslovakia and Eire.

LAMBS TO THE SLAUGHTER

Now it has to be said that most attempts to impose a campaign developed in one country on another are received with about as much enthusiasm as British lamb by French farmers: the trucks are seized and the contents burned. This is, in many respects, understandable. Marketers are executives and executives enjoy – and some are good at – wielding power. The origination, development and positive evaluation of an advertising campaign are very distinct manifestations – often the chief expression – of that power. And few marketers are consequently likely to welcome what clearly amounts to some sort of quite serious emasculation of that power. The advertising agency in the local market – whether or not it is part of the same network as the home agency – is likely to be similarly displeased. Advertising imposed from abroad is inevitably seen as an implicit criticism of its own work and, even if the agency continues to buy the media for the campaign, it is likely to suffer financially. Disappointingly few advertisers will pay for creativity if all they need is media-buying. The instinctive response of the local distributor and the agency is thus almost invariably negative. They are losing part or all of their jobs.

Given that this will be the attitude adopted, the players then cast around for some good reasons. Many of these will seem persuasive. The brand is a market-leader at home and an also-ran abroad. The campaign is a predominantly verbal one which translates poorly. Its main media is TV, but local advertising legislation forbids the promotion of the product in that medium; the work is humorous and, as everyone knows, the French have no sense of humour . . . It is this attitude and these sorts of arguments that should make marketing people with a degree of common sense ponder the pros and cons of exporting campaigns quite carefully.

Superficially, the argument in favour of so doing is one of cost. Developing advertising is at best an expensive business and the costs are not simply those of the agency's sizeable invoice. There is also the matter your management time as an advertiser. It would thus appear to follow that if you do have something that in advertising is rare – a very good idea – it should be used as widely as possible. It saves the money of originating a new one for each of the main markets, and it also saves some of the production costs. For the tidy-minded there is also a certain neatness in such uniformity of presentation, something that might even be noticed by the very small but growing number of international travellers who normally see different advertising for the same brand in different countries. A company spending $100m in three countries might, theoretically, expect to save perhaps $7m in agency fees by consolidating the work into a single agency. Or perhaps $5m by imposing uniform strategies and creative work on incumbent agencies, retaining them in local markets for tactical work, media buying and taking the marketing director out to lunch. In the percentage game that businesses are in, this is a small but significant and quite tangible saving. Saving the company $5m looks good on anyone's CV.

This practical argument – it has to be said by no means invariably validated by experience – is normally buttressed by something more theoretical. Many multinational corporations take the 'global approach' as more or less an article of faith. Survival depends on survival in the global market-place, competing with other global players in pursuit of the phantasmic global consumer. All other aspects of the company's business are based on this premise, so why not marketing? Moreover, it is not simply a question of the will of the company. The world itself is converging and compressing, becoming daily more homogeneous in its wants and needs. McDonalds are now in Moscow; soon, doubtless, they will be in Peking. National marketing is reactionary; global marketing is the way ahead. It is even, in fact, possible today. It is so in organisational terms: other people do it; it is so in practical terms – look at Esso and Coke; and it is increasingly so in media terms. There are already international advertising vehicles both in print and TV and in due course these will doubtless become global.

However, it is clear enough that cost of one nature or another is also the downside. Given that it is more than possible for advertising to make or break brands, it rather behoves a company to ensure that it gets the best possible advertising for its brands in all its markets. And, as this book argues, best means most appropriate. Or rather, most appropriate means best. The upside of a central marketing saving therefore has to be balanced against the risk of running advertising that is, if not normally inappropriate, then at least not as appropriate as it could be. And it is here that central marketing departments, however organised, have to make difficult, judgemental and frequently unpopular decisions.

STRATEGIC SIMILARITIES

Given this not altogether encouraging context, your first job is to look at the status of the brand in the local market and take a view on advertising strategy.

This can be a fascinating exercise because of the extent to which it illustrates the way in which the same thing can be seen in a quite different way by the same sort of people in different places; or to put it another way, because it illustrates how effectively certain aspects of marketing theory actually work in practice. Take the lager Stella Artois, and Mercedes cars. It is an exaggeration to say that these are staples in their home markets of Belgium and Germany and purely premium brands where they're marketed abroad, but there's still a fair measure of truth in it. Marketing has persuaded local targets that these are special brands for which it's worth paying quite a lot extra.

Brands like this with *radically different positionings in different national markets* are the exception rather than the rule, but it's probably fair to say that brands with *different positionings in different markets* are the rule rather than the exception. The day of the simultaneous global, or at least international, launch of a brand will undoubtedly come, but it isn't here yet. This means that at least at the moment brands have starting-places – normally home countries – where virtually by definition they have a certain status: they're home-grown and they've been around for some time. However, when the same brand is exported, it is precisely that status that it can't assume: it is not home-grown and it hasn't been around. This means that it is likely to enjoy a different status abroad to the status it enjoys at home – although it might reasonably follow that it possessed a similar position among the various different countries where it enjoyed export status. Clearly, Gordon's London Gin won't be seen in the same light in California as it is in Great Britain. Conversely, it might theoretically be similarly viewed in Tahiti and Timbuktu. Actually even this doesn't necessarily follow. It is still relatively unusual to launch a brand simultaneously in several countries abroad, so differences are likely to arise as a consequence of the brand's apparent age and the extent to which it has become established. The case of Ford is instanced in Nükhet Vandar's *Global Advertising*, with an account director working on the business remarking: 'Ford is an interesting case, because they sell the same cars everywhere. In Spain we are considered gay and dynamic. In France, boring. In Italy, simply a car for people who can't afford Fiats.'

This all means that for those seeking differences in brand positioning, differences are there to be found and they are certainly the sorts of differences that affect advertising strategy. Or should do anyway.

Those who are familiar with international departure lounges will certainly accept that such differences exist, but will argue that *the differences are less important than the similarities*. This isn't in fact so unreasonable. Whatever the nature of competitive products, a power-drill in Holland is pretty much the same power-drill in Spain: it looks the same, feels the same and is used in much the same way. Then, of course, the nature of the product dictates the nature of the brand. True, there may be tonal differences, or differences of nuance and attitude, but the *thing* is essentially the same. There are one or two entertaining instances where it's necessary to change a brand's name for it to operate in a foreign market, but generally these too are constants. So too is the packaging, on which some brands depend for their identity. Such things as distribution, market share, and share-of-voice doubtless differ, but the heart of the brand remains the same. And if the heart is the same, so too should surely be the brand's most public face, its advertising.

Needless to say, there is no universal resolution to this argument, the answer depending very largely on the brand and product under discussion. As far as strategy goes, it is unlikely to be very appropriate to use the same message in market-places where the same brand has radically different positionings. That's simple. More difficult, equally clearly, is to decide if the brand is in a position in which the differences that are invariably present are indeed outweighed by the similarities. Consumer research in the local market can clearly help here, although the standard of such work even within Europe is quite variable, albeit improving. Equally, you're likely to be swayed by something that may or may not come with a uniform strategy, perhaps dictated for reasons of dogma from head office: uniform creative work. If there is evidence that the creativity has worked excellently else-where, then many may well feel it sensible to decide that, in this particular instance, the similarities in positioning are indeed greater than the differences.

The first thing to do in any case is to pigeon-hole the positioning of the brand. Figure 11.2 shows the holes.

Market	Product	Distribution	Price	Promotion	Consumer
Home					
Local 1					
Local 2					
Local 3					

Figure 11.2   Home and away: analysing the brand's international profile

CREATIVE DIFFERENCES

The truth ultimately may well of course be that a brand is a brand is a brand, and that as the markets in which it operates mature, communications develop, desires converge etc., a degree of convergence between its positioning in different countries is in practice more than likely. This really shifts the balance in favour of some degree of international coherence of strategy, or at the very least gradual moves towards such a common goal. However, it is by no means clear that the same argument applies equally to creativity.

Perhaps the essence of effective creative work is that it shows that the advertiser understands its consumers: it demonstrates that the brand owner grasps the circumstances in which the brand is bought or used, why it's bought and who buys it, and presents these things to potential buyers in a sympathetic matter. The advertiser manifests empathy with consumers; the buyers identify with – often aspire to – their idealized portraits. This all sounds very attractive and agreeable, but it is clear enough that the one thing on which the whole splendid edifice is built is the idea of understanding. Now assuming that the original campaign was competently developed, the ad or campaign may very well manifest exactly the required comprehension of its target . . . in the home market. The snag that arises is, of course, that in the same way as the status of brands varies from market to market, so too, very often, does the nature of consumers. Potential buyers in different countries come from different backgrounds, enjoy different cultures and, as a consequence, respond to the same advertising in different ways.

In practice, advertising ideas that travel effectively are, broadly speaking, those that of course translate, but translate both literally and metaphorically. The literal side is fairly easy. Advertising ideas can very loosely be categorised as visual or verbal, and it is obvious that the former tend to be more suited for export than the latter. Verbally-based advertising ideas often depend on plays on words, or words grouped together as much for their *sound* as their sense. Such ideas suffer in translation.

The metaphorical issue is rather more judgemental. One quite useful way of looking at advertising is that it is centrally concerned with comparisons – metaphors and similes. Brands in themselves – lavatory paper, washing-up liquid – tend to be pretty unexciting things, and it is one of the strengths of advertising that by dramatising what a brand is *like* rather than what it *is*, it can convey an infinitely more appealing image. The skill of the agency then lies in doing two things: finding a metaphor that is appropriate for the brand; and ensuring that the metaphor means what it is intended to mean to buyers. The problem lies in the fact that while there are a number of images and symbols that mean more or less the same thing in different countries, there are many that don't. The cross is a symbol of consistent value and meaning in Christendom but less satisfactory outside it; Michael Jackson's image is probably uniform except among those who feel that he's abandoned his own race; the Red Crescent still means little as a symbol in the west; white in China is the colour of mourning.

If the idea is to work then, it must clearly translate. Or to put it another way, if you are developing a campaign to run outside the home market it is crucial to put yourself in the position of your buyers abroad and ensure that what you imagine an advertising idea means is something that they share. Again, consumer research can help here, as can common sense.

Then there's the issue of the manifestation of this idea. Manifestations matter. Indeed it could be said in advertising that little else matters. Although quite a lot has been written here about advertising ideas, the reality is that the idea is often less important that its manifestation. An idea might involve the notion of an Englishman abroad, or – say – an American in

Paris. Sufficiently familiar ideas, even clichés. There is little doubt that people do react to these ideas, but they really react much more to their physical manifestations in terms of casting, setting and, more generally, production values. This means that although a James Bond film is a James Bond film, people undoubtedly react differently to – respectively – Sean Connery, George Lazenby, Roger Moore and Timothy Dalton. The consequence of this for advertisers is often awkward. Even given the same script, an advertising agency in Ajaccio would undoubtedly cast, dress and set a commercial in a significantly different way to its equivalent in Amsterdam. And, equally, people will notice these differences. If advertising seeks to establish an identity of sentiment or lifestyle between advertiser and consumer, it is exactly these matters of detail that are so important. Images of – say, manhood, womanhood and childhood – from country to country undoubtedly differ. Over-dubbing a commercial with English voices is by no means the solution for audiences who are as advertising literate as is these days normally the case.

Finally, it's worth adding that there is clear evidence that different cultures have different expectations from and bring different expectations to advertising. Americans really do expect a relatively direct sell from their advertising, meaning that it often comprises an explicit, rational selling proposition, sometimes at a specific price, and occasionally compared with named competitive products. It is the language of the market-place, or even the bazaar. Conversely, Anglo-Saxon – in the sense of English, Australian etc. – ads tend to use a softer sell approach, based more on the imagery of the brand. Europe – or, rather, different countries within it – is different again. The French use sex to sell everything – even kitchen tiles; the Swiss – as befits that temperate people – normally don't; what used to be the eastern bloc is quite unfamiliar with the 'language' of western advertising and can react in unexpected ways to it. These differences matter.

This isn't, of course, to say that there are no circumstances in which it is ever sensible to run creative work developed for one country in another. Rather, that you need to conduct a fairly rigorous process of appraisal of the status of the brand in the market, the nature of the consumer in the context of the given product sector, and the nature of the creative idea. Where a brand enjoys a status in its local market that is not too dissimilar from its status at home, where consumers' feelings about the product are broadly comparable, and where an excellent idea exists which will translate, the cost argument in favour of common origination and production is powerful. The truth is that these circumstances are rare, although – as national brands become international brands – they are increasing. Nükhet

Vandar reports that McCann Ericksen – with considerable experience in international advertising – takes the following view:

1 Marketing standardisation works best when the brand is:
   - contemporary, international, fashionable;
   - marketed at similar price levels to similar audiences;
   - has similar patterns of consumption patterns;
   - is youth orientated;
   - is an indulgence product, not a necessity.

2 Advertising centralisation works best when the campaign:
   - has a strong creative idea;
   - is not dependent on price or promotion;
   - avoids local personalities, models etc.;
   - has a strong brand property.

These points are at least worth considering.

MEDIA

Before your campaign – centralised or otherwise – gets under way, the final issue to tackle is media. Now if the political, strategic and creative issues in advertising abroad are sufficiently complex, media is, if anything, more so. Agonising over the work is all of little moment if the right people aren't reached at a reasonable cost, and of course actually placing the work in the consumer's eye is the single largest cost associated with advertising. It has to be right. Circumstances unfortunately conspire against this. The media arrangements in any given country in the last decade of the twentieth century are likely to be sufficiently complex. The troubles then are three. Media differs significantly from country to country, the idea of a relatively fixed rate-card applies by no means universally, and the standards of media research – providing quite useful information on who consumes what – are very variable.

For those familiar with a dozen or so national newspapers, three or four TV stations forever at each other's throats, hundreds of consumer magazines, and a fast-developing commercial radio network, the arrangements in other countries can come as a bit of a shock. Everyone knows there are dozens of television channels in America, but the absence of national newspapers there and – effectively – in most of continental Europe – tends to come as a surprise. Equally, even where national commercial TV stations exist – and in Scandinavia they still don't – television air-time can be in short supply and funds have to be committed months rather than weeks in advance. If, somehow, you can select a medium, the audience that it enjoys is often harder than you might expect to define, readership and circulation figures being, apparently, not altogether susceptible to translation. This, in turn, makes assessing the value – and hence price – of a given medium doubly difficult, the 'rate-card' sometimes being definable as the highest sum the media-owner can get the advertiser to pay.

These are genuinely difficult problems. Sorting out where a brand stands in the market-place, what its consumers are like and what advertising is likely to work involves a certain amount of time, trouble and effort, but is certainly within the compass of a competent, centralised marketing depart-ment. A familiarity with the intricacies of the media market in these countries is not. This really forces the brand owner back into the hands of the local agency on the grounds that – particularly in the media arena – it will undoubtedly have sufficient local knowledge. Ultimately this imperative is expensive and involved. It requires the establishment and maintenance of a series of contacts in local markets at a time at which the need to use the other services, particularly creativity, is often diminishing. The international offices of the larger international agencies may offer some competition, and may indeed offer adequate local advice through a network. But ultimately the chances of getting the media value you get in the home market abroad are limited.

The table below shows the considerable variations in media structure that exist even across Europe.

Table 11.1 Media across Europe

Country	Press	TV	Radio	Other
	%	%	%	%
Austria	51.3	28.3	12.6	7.8
Belgium	55.1	25.9	0.9	18.1
Denmark	86.7	9.0	1.9	2.4
Finland	80.3	13.4	3.6	2.8
France	50.7	27.8	7.6	13.9
Germany	74.7	14.6	5.3	5.3
Greece	45.1	40.8	7.3	6.8
Ireland	54.1	28.9	10.0	6.9
Italy	42.7	51.5	1.6	4.1
Netherlands	72.3	12.1	2.3	13.3
Norway	94.3	1.6	0.8	3.3
Portugal	37.5	48.2	8.9	5.4
Spain	52.8	30.1	11.1	5.9
Sweden	94.4	–	–	5.6
Switzerland	65.2	7.7	2.0	15.0
UK	52.6	39.8	2.5	5.2

© *The European Marketing Pocket Book*, NTC Publications Ltd.

ADVERTISING EVALUATION

One of the major themes of this book has been the importance of improving the ways in which advertising is evaluated and, as a consequence, ultimately improving the creative product. As has been stressed, measuring the impact of advertising is difficult in the best of circumstances and, clearly, advertising abroad for most brand owners rarely approaches that best. This means that if the quality of advertising evaluation in the home market rarely rises above the indifferent, abroad it ranges from the primitive to the poor.

This is largely but not entirely intrinsic to the fact of running campaigns in several different countries. As has been argued, the only real way of measuring advertising is to track all the other major influences on the market-place, overlay the advertising campaign, and try to isolate advertising effects. This is quite a business in one country, let alone several, and few companies make any very serious efforts along these lines. Perhaps that's a little unfair. The majority satisfy themselves that the campaign is running well somewhere and assume – or hope – that the impact is replicated elsewhere. This is understandable in so far as even the half-way house of 'surrogate' measures of things like advertising awareness are quite difficult to achieve. Many companies advertising in different markets do try this approach, and it's undoubtedly better than nothing. Most take the form of an 'international tracking study'. These are difficult to set up, manage and interpret because of – as ever – the inconsistencies between countries.

This starts with the survey questionnaire. While it is possible for simple issues like advertising awareness and recognition to be tracked consistently through a multinational sample, more subjective and complex ones like brand imagery are more difficult because of the problems of accurate translation. A poor score on the attitude of – say – 'modernity' in one country may be attributable to the value or slightly different meaning of the local word, rather than a problem with the brand or its advertising. Even if some linguistic consistency is achieved, the varying standard of fieldwork in different countries can skew results quite significantly. Market research personnel differ considerably in their ardour for accurate samples, and certain European and South American countries are notoriously poor. Moreover, in the same way as different cultures come to the advertising itself with different expectations, so too do they come to market research. The tradition of demographic institutions means that in certain countries people are very familiar with having their opinions canvassed. Equally there are others – notably in eastern europe – where such procedures and institutions are rather more novel. This not unnaturally affects the way questions are answered.

This all puts a series of question-marks over interpretation that inevitably exists anyway. Tracking studies are sources of information that are almost entirely meaningless unless they are set in the context of such data as distribution, market share and advertising share-of-voice. And as this information is by no means invariably available to advertisers, it is usually difficult to say what the tracking means. Add to this the limitations of 'surrogate' measures discussed elsewhere, then it follows that this sort of work more than ever is *indicative* of advertising impact, rather than anything closely related to how or whether it really is working.

HOW TO ADVERTISE ABROAD

Advertising abroad is a tricky business. Its first principle, naturally enough, must be the same as that for advertising in the home market: that the work used is the most appropriate that can be contrived for the brand, its situation in the market, its consumers, and of course the brand's marketing objectives. Key word: appropriate. The snag is that while it is difficult enough to develop appropriate advertising in the home market, company culture and organisation on the one hand, the differences between the markets home and abroad on the other, make the job of getting the right work in foreign markets even more challenging. In these circumstances it's tempting to do one of two things:

- to wash your hands of the whole business and let the locals get on with it;
- to impose everywhere Saatchi's jolly successful Swedish campaign, willy-nilly.

Now, while either of these approaches may turn out to provide each market with its most appropriate advertising, neither is very likely to do so. The consequence is that really the only way to advertise effectively in foreign markets is to stick to the principle of appropriateness. This means, in practice, doing two things. It means casting aside – or at least working round – political pressures to follow precept or prejudice; and instead conducting a thorough and time-consuming review of brand strategy, creativity and consumers in the local markets. Only then are you in a position to decide what sort of advertising is right, and whether it conforms with corporate prejudice.

CASE HISTORY 5
Absolut Success – The Story of Absolut Vodka

Sweden's Absolut Vodka is a case-history of consistent marketing and advertising across what now amounts to seventy different countries, ranging from Norway to the West Indies.

Simply as a brand, Absolut has an interesting history. Vodka has been produced in Sweden since the fifteenth century, using as its base either grain or potatoes. The appeal of the final product depends partly on its alcoholic strength, but ultimately on its purity, the genius here being L. O. Smith, one of Sweden's nineteenth-century '*brannvin*' – burnt or distilled wine – 'kings'. In 1879 he produced a uniquely pure potato vodka dubbed 'absolutely pure *brannvin*'. This provided the starting-point for the Swedish state drinks monopoly Vin & Sprit when, in the early 1970s, it began seeking major international business by way of an export vodka. The requirement was for something which could genuinely excel in a heavily branded market where perceived product differences were few. This dictated replacing Smith's potatoes with grain, and a stringent process which created a vodka with significantly fewer impurities – and thus a significantly cleaner taste – than the competition. It was appropriately branded Absolut Vodka, and marketed in a modernised version of an old Swedish medicine bottle.

The idea was to launch it not in its home market, but in the country which accounts for 60 per cent of western vodka consumption – the US. To this end, Vin & Sprit went into partnership with Carillon, then a small distributor which had distinguished itself by using new and unconventional methods to launch brands, most notably Grand Marnier. Together, the two companies conducted what was intended to be concept and product fine-tuning research – with relatively poor results. Absolut looked like nothing else on the market; its purity suggested the sterile and clinical; its name couldn't be read against the transparent contents; consumers wouldn't notice the bottle on the shelf etc., etc.

In the marketing world the rest is history.

Despite those findings, the brand was launched in Boston in 1979. In its first year it sold 10,000 cases, by its second 100,000; by 1985 it had overtaken the Russian Stolichnaya to become the largest brand of imported vodka in the US; by 1987 it was selling 1.4 million cases; by 1990 it was the biggest imported *spirit* in the country with sales of over 2 million; and sales today stand at 2.6 million.

Advertising is accepted to have played a major part in this success. Originated by TBWA New York in 1980, the thinking was that spirits' advertising was generic, dominated by beautiful settings, elegant people, and bold promises about product superiority. The Absolut work was to contrast starkly by concentrating single-mindedly on the product – arguably the brand – each shot showing the bottle. The headlines would then vary the Absolut theme: Absolut Perfection showed the bottle topped with a halo; in Absolut Elegance it wore a black tie. With no overt product claim or user-imagery, the campaign seemed to work for four reasons:

- its wit and intelligence is tightly focused on the brand's target – well described by V&S as 'well-educated, high-income earners in information intensive, major metropolitan markets';
- it also focuses on the brand's USP purity, ultimately a by-word for strength;
- it is very heavily branded;
- it has been used over the years with great consistency.

The job then was for V&S to repeat this success in its other countries. This was an interesting challenge because the markets are in many respects as diverse as might be expected. For instance, spirits generally are big business in Germany with an average per capita consumption of 5.2 litres of alcohol. In Australia the figure is 1.2 litres. In the UK white spirits take just about a third of the spirits market and vodka slightly less than half that; in France white spirits take 2.25 per cent of the spirits market. In the UK vodka has a brash young image; in Spain this belongs to gin. In the UK vodka is the largest growing spirit, now bigger than gin; in Italy consumption is 'marginal'.

Superficially, this is a recipe for confusion and so in a sense it is. Absolut is operating in markets with diverse volumes, levels of maturity, sector consumer images. There is therefore inevitably a temptation to let the local importers have their heads and prepare marketing and advertising quite precisely created for the particular market. The temptation is to let the differences between markets prevail.

In practice this has been resisted by V&S. Its argument is that despite the sort of differences listed above, the job in most markets is effectively the same: there are few perceived product differences between the various brands, so the objective for Absolut is always to create a new premium sector among a target internationally relatively homogeneous: well-educated, high-income earners in information intensive, major metropolitan markets . . . It follows that while local distributors are permitted a degree of latitude in marketing arrangements, high levels of consistency are achieved by way of pricing (inevitably premium), distribution (upscale restaurants, bars and hotels) and advertising. The basic TBWA concept – often existing TBWA New York ads – is very easily adaptable to other languages.

In most of these markets it is too early to make definitive assessments of the success of this approach. Nevertheless, in Greece, Canada and France the signs are that this internationally consistent marketing and advertising programme is now beginning to reap rewards.

CHECKLIST

1 The nature of the advertising run in foreign markets is first and foremost a function of company culture and organisation. Make sure you know exactly what this is before doing anything rash.

2 The practical key to advertising outside the home market lies in getting to know the differences between home and local markets, and deciding which it is possible to ignore, and which need to be taken into account.

3 Given the rarity of good advertising ideas and the cost of developing advertising of any nature, it is very tempting to try to export advertising. This will usually be resisted by the local operators.

4 The job then is to decide whether reasons of self-interest or rather better ones prevail. This means first looking at the relative positioning of the brands in their market. There are three basic categories: those brands with radically different positionings at home and abroad; those with comparable positionings; and the majority betwixt and between.

5 If the positioning is radically different, it is likely to be necessary to use a different advertising strategy and different advertising. If comparable, then the same strategy may be usable. In the majority of cases it is necessary to decide whether the similarities in positioning outweigh the differences, justifying the same strategy.

6 Often the arguments in favour of a uniform strategy are strong. The need for creative work to have high levels of empathy with its target means that those in favour of uniform creativity are generally less so.

7 The most effective option in buying media is to use local agencies.

8 Basic tracking studies for evaluating advertising in local markets are better than nothing.

12 IRRECONCILABLE DIFFERENCES
Managing the client/agency relationship

'You treat me badly'
Atwater said: 'Men do treat women badly. You must have discovered that by now.'

ANTHONY POWELL
Afternoon Men

Agency/client relationships difficult · quality of relationship key to good advertising · agencies and advertisers both to blame · ways of managing agencies · advertising executives human · ways of managing clients · advertising managers human · building relationships · temptation to sack the agency · why it should be resisted · when it shouldn't.

You have now come a long, long way with your agency. You have vetted and hired it; set objectives, discussed strategies and extracted – at length – the creative work; you have argued over media and a ludicrous proposal on advertorials; you nearly came to blows over the production estimate; and you were actually struck and quite severely injured by the commercial's director, who thought you interfering. The material finally produced seemed OK. Did it work? Perhaps; but really it is too early to tell. The marketing director was sufficiently pleased to try to foist it on the French, who at length accepted it with ill-grace . . .

The truth is that trying to get advertising, or rather good advertising, out of any agency is a tough job and having come such a way with the agency you may now well feel that, in fact, you have come far enough. For other than that between prostitute and pimp there is perhaps no relationship in the business world so fraught as that between an advertiser and its agency. If advertisers do stay with agencies for years rather than months, then they don't stay for many. A significant number of liaisons do only last for months; and weeks or days is not uncommon. It is a volatile world.

Quite why is rather less clear. Perhaps it stems intrinsically from the difficulty of objectively analysing an agency's performance. It is tricky to tell how good any advertising is, and some agencies have been singular in their failure to make their efforts more accountable. This clearly puts the client/ agency relationship on a different footing to that between a manufacturer and its component suppliers, distributors, lawyers and accountants, all of whose contributions can be measured, if not quite objectively, then at least slightly more so than that of an agency. Agencies are very rarely sacked because the advertising isn't working. They are more often dismissed because it is *imagined* not be working. This tends to shift the basis of assessment into the definitively subjective area of personal relationships – whether or not the advertiser likes and trusts the agency people – and it is here of course that agencies sometimes do themselves disservice. Despite all the talk of business partnership between the two sides, some agency people seem to regard their clients as a lower, almost sub-human species; and don't take many pains to conceal this attitude. This perspective – not always justifiable – is perhaps an unconscious expression of the resentment some feel as a consequence of their supplier status. 'I wince whenever I hear the word supplier applied to the client/agency relationship', remarks the London chairman of a large international agency. This is typical. Advertising people are uncomfortable about a situation in which they are judged by those who some imagine to be their social, economic and intellectual inferiors. And the resentment shows.

This isn't something that greatly enhances the relationship, yet agency indulgence can go further. If agencies patronise their clients they also sometimes exploit them, take insufficient trouble to conceal this exploitation, and indeed are positively ostentatious about their level of profiteering. Advertising in the past has been a profitable business, in some instances highly so. It remains so in some countries, and to an extent the good times will doubtless return. This is partly because the acknowledged profit margins at least used to be reasonably high, and partly because some agencies also make more money than they are supposed to acting as middlemen between clients and the various suppliers to the advertising business, notably media and production. While such agencies naturally make attempts to conceal this from their clients, marketing directors are often aware that this happens, the only question lying in the extent to which it is conducted by a particular agency at a particular time. This too, is something that scarcely fosters a mutual trust and understanding that should be natural between business partners. Then, having made quite a lot of money out of their clients and paying their personnel quite highly in relation to their talents, there's the ostentatious parading of this wealth in the form of Rolexes, Porsches and sharp suits. The irony here is that advertising people are actually paid significantly less than their contemporaries in such outwardly more respectable professions as law, accountancy and merchant banking. The difference is that the latter are discreet in their displays of wealth. Advertising has only itself to blame for the perception that its practitioners are overpaid. And it can hardly be surprised that this too is something that its clients resent.

Of course, all these things – and it should be stressed that these represent only the worst possible cases – would be of little moment if the quality of the relationship between an agency and its client, an advertiser and its agency, didn't matter. However it does. On a purely practical level even the largest of agencies are relatively small businesses and losing an account is a serious issue; equally agencies are king-makers, sometimes capable of making and breaking their clients' careers. Moreover, if the relationship matters, its quality is really crucial. Much in the way that agencies sometimes behave militates against the establishment of confidence, trust and respect, yet paradoxically it is precisely those attitudes that are so important in producing good advertising. Creating advertising is inevitably a collective effort between advertisers whose job is the marketing of brands, and agencies whose job is their advertising. In this sense it *is* a partnership, but a partnership of people enjoying not so much unequal, but different skills. In this situation, unless each partner has a degree of respect for the other's particular area of expertise, little can be achieved. The best results occur when each partner acknowledges the limitations of their experience and is prepared to take a risk on that basis, accepting the professional advice of their consultants. Often the reverse occurs, the advertiser hiring a dog and then barking himself. This is a shame because effective communication and, in particular, effective advertising very often involves doing things differently to the way in which they've been done before – because if they are not, no one will notice what the advertiser is saying. Generally speaking, this means that the onus falls on marketing directors and brand managers to take risks. Equally, the responsibility falls on agencies to do what they're sometimes poor at doing: establishing a relationship that gives their clients the confidence to take those risks. As Peter Mead, the president of the British IPA puts it, 'Our aim is to destroy the view that advertising is a commodity. It is the creation of an elusive spark of originality which can fundamentally enhance a client's business. But in order to create that elusive spark, the relationship between client and agency has to be on a firm footing, embracing both respect and trust.'

MANAGING THE AGENCY

From your point of view as an advertiser, it follows that while it's a good idea to choose the right agency, oversee the strategy, keep the media department on its toes and so on, in many respects the most difficult yet most important part of the business of getting decent advertising lies in the more general business of the day-to-day management of the agency. And if the drift of this chapter so far has been the sometimes generous contributions of agencies themselves to the poverty of their relationship with clients, it's safe to say that some on the client side manage to reciprocate quite fully. There are four chief ways to improve that situation.

Keep on briefing

It is clear enough that the quality or otherwise of the advertising any agency produces is more or less dependent on the quality of the briefing, but this awareness is not invariably followed through.

Briefing is in fact a continuous process that takes two forms: the communication of fact; and the communication of opinion. Facts are for advertising agencies, as much as for manufacturers and service companies, valuable commodities. Advertising is the tip of the marketing iceberg and it follows that agencies do need to know, and know on a regular basis, a proportion of the information that competent marketing departments collect as a matter of course. It encourages them to think about the advertising in the way it should be thought of: in the context of the brand, competitive activity, and such issues as product development, pricing fluctuations, and distribution gains and losses. It is absurd to suggest that agencies need to know this sort of thing in the detail that marketing departments themselves require. It is equally absurd to believe that effective advertising can be developed in ignorance of such information, or at least the understanding to which a knowledge of this information leads. Some advertisers appear to take the view that agencies are not to be trusted with this sort of information, and if they are, then not much of it. If that is the case they can also be trusted to produce advertising that is inappropriate to the brand's situation. The second sort of briefing is really a corollary of the first. If agencies need information to develop and continually update their understanding of a brand, you need equally to keep them abreast of your own and your company's opinion of the brand's status – and accordingly the needs of advertising. This seems trite enough and is indeed the substance of many day-to-day conversations between marketing and account directors.

The real problem lies elsewhere. As agencies are all too vividly aware, there are a number of people both inside and outside marketing departments who have views on their company's advertising and whose opinions matter – usually the sales director and the managing director. Marketing directors occasionally seem to see these colleagues as innocents whose virginity about advertising people, and as far as possible advertising, it is wise to preserve. Ultimately this is counter-productive. Agencies need regular contact with everyone in their client company whose opinions on the advertising count.

Sitting in judgement

The reciprocal process to putting information and opinion into an agency is getting some work out – be it a creative brief, a media schedule, a trade ad or a major new campaign. Judging this work – particularly creative work – is a particularly difficult job, as is the broader one which it implicitly involves: extracting the best possible work from the people who work on the business.

The starting-point here has to be that agencies are sometimes lazy, often under-staffed, and certainly don't have a monopoly of wisdom. This means that they occasionally have to be coerced, cajoled, bullied and flattered into doing the work – or rather the extra work that makes the difference between the adequate and the good. It is worth remembering that generally the best agency staff choose to work on a particular piece of business rather than being obliged to do so. This places a significant onus on you as an advertiser to employ conventional management skills on agency staff to get the work done. Sometimes rather the opposite process occurs. The situation also means that the work produced won't invariably be right. Agency people are as capable as anyone else of making elementary mistakes and neglecting crucial pieces of information. They can also quite simply be wrong.

That said, advertising people are what marketing people by definition are not: advertising specialists. Wisdom suggests that there is indeed little point in buying a dog and barking yourself. Although agencies don't invariably do a great deal to inculcate trust and respect, there's really very little logic in having one if the advertising generally reflects the prejudices of the marketing department more than it does those of the agency. Prejudices are prejudices, but in communication matters the agency's should prevail. As Robert Townsend recorded in his book *Up the Organisation*, on the process of producing the famous Avis 'We try Harder' campaign, the cardinal rules governing the relationship between agency and client were:

1 Doyle Dane Bernbach will never know as much about car-rental as Avis;
2 Avis will never know as much about advertising as Doyle Dane Bernbach.

This seems such a rational position as scarcely to merit expression. It is mentioned because too often it's the exception rather than the rule. If you don't trust the people who are supposed to advise you on communication matters, find someone you do. Or go into advertising yourself.

Who will guard the guardians?

If it was as easy to say 'yes' to advertising as it is to another drink, there would be little difficulty in the marketing director's or the agency's job – and perhaps little interest. Judging advertising is not easy for anyone, but client approval processes occasionally give agencies the impression that they'd be better employed easing camels through the eyes of needles than getting work approved. Some advertisers have labyrinthine approval systems the entrances and exits to which marketing departments guard from their agencies with great vigour. This is depressing. Agencies need simple approval procedures and should be given the facility of presenting work at senior level. It's also important – as has been suggested elsewhere – that no arbitrary pre-testing system is imposed on the work.

In practice, getting approval for work – particularly in large firms – can be infinitely time-consuming and infinitely frustrating. There is nothing more demotivating for agencies than to have work turned down from on high for what invariably seem whimsical reasons. It is an agency joke that work risks being rejected because the chairman's wife dislikes it. It is less of a joke when this actually happens. And it does.

Advertising agents are human (too)

The final point worth making is that it's really in the advertiser's interest to think of the people they deal with less as account executives, art directors or media planners, but as human beings. It is very easy to slip into the mode of thought that regards each agency representative as an automaton, mechanically, effortlessly, unerringly and continuously working on your behalf. The job does to an extent require them to be so, but if they actually are to perform in such a way, it's useful to think of them as entities with lives outside the agency, opinions that the politics of client/agency relationships forbids expression and, perhaps above all, as people who need to be motivated to work on your behalf. A commonplace incident is the occasion on which the client phones to complain about some piece of work done badly or not done at all, prefacing – and following – the remarks with the observation that 'We pay you $40,000 a month to do this.' For many agency executives this argument is beside the point. It is the agency, not the executives themselves who are being paid $40,000 a month; they don't just work on your account; and though partly, they are not entirely motivated by money. What does motivate them? The answer is the sense of doing a good job, the sense of this being recognised, the respect of their peers within the agency, fun, and sometimes 'good' advertising. Some also wish to advance their careers; some to go home and spend more time with their families; some to go to an hotel and spend more time with their mistresses. Perhaps some of these ambitions are more laudable than others, but all – to a lesser or greater extent – play a part in the ad-man's make up. Sensitive management perhaps requires the appreciation that the ad-man's agenda isn't invariably quite what the advertiser might require or expect.

It's worth adding that – contrary to appearances – many ad people are (in certain respects) quite vulnerable. By comparison with a job like – say – fund management, the objective assessment of executives' performance is impossible. You just can't say that Jim Ring has earned the agency $100,000 in the last six months. There are some in new business circles who will attempt to take such credit, but both the business of winning pitches and producing advertising generally is too collective an act for anyone really to be singled out for credit – or blame. And as the advertising itself can't be objectively assessed, most ad people aren't judged on whether they are associated in any way with advertising that works, but on what their colleagues and, above all, what their clients think of them. This, of course, makes advertising agencies the political organisations they are, and also means that people's bonuses, promotions and careers are peculiarly susceptible to client comment. In this respect ad people are highly vulnerable.

MANAGING THE CLIENT

If advertisers concern themselves spasmodically with the issue of nurturing their relationship with the agency having a view to improving the quality of the work so produced, so too do agencies. Spasmodically. Accounts aren't always run with a view to getting the best possible advertising. They can be managed defensively to retain the account or offensively to be as profitable as possible. For a few agencies attractive and effective advertising sometimes seems to be an agreeable by-product of their work rather than a *raison d'être*. Agencies after all are businesses. This view may be short-sighted but it is now nevertheless not altogether uncommon. Of course, advertisers must themselves shoulder some of the blame here, because of the ways already indicated in which they sometimes stand in the way of 'good' advertising. But agencies, both in terms of their general attitudes and specific actions, equally sometimes do little themselves for the great cause. Again, leaving aside the points raised in Chapters 5, 6, 7 and 8, it is perhaps possible to suggest one or two ways of managing clients in a way which contributes towards the quality of the work rather than arguing against it.

Getting to know you

Advertising is a specialised business but it is also an intrinsic part of the marketing process. Agencies sometimes seem to find this point difficult to grasp, living in a largely self-referential world of creative briefs, media schedules and post-production houses in the more attractive parts of capital cities. This isn't in the end what marketing is about and in particular it has very little to do with the way in which clients, on a day-to-day basis, involve themselves with the brand that it's the agency's job to help to sell. Hands-on marketing is about the realities of persuading an overworked R & D depart-ment to come up with a decent product spec, trying to achieve half-way reasonable distribution on a product that clearly isn't sufficiently supported, and struggling for the consumer's attention in a painfully crowded market-place. It is clearly naïve for advertisers to expect their agencies – in a phrase by no means infrequently used – to know more about their business than they do themselves. Equally, it is simply not possible to produce appropriate and therefore effective advertising if agencies aren't in possession of the sort of knowledge that comes from what might be described as experiencing a brand rather than reading about it. Talking to the people who make the product, those who distribute it, and those who buy it – even buying it and using it yourself – is an obvious way to do this. Not enough agencies seem to do this in much more than a fairly cursory manner, partly because they are busy on other accounts, partly because such activities are seen as being in some way peripheral to the business of producing ads. Far from peripheral, they are in fact central, with much of the worst advertising of the past decade arguably arising because of the extent to which the work is divorced from the everyday realities of the consumer's experience of the brand.

Not invented here

Marketing can in many respects be a very frustrating job because of the contrast that it offers between the theory of manipulating product, price, distribution and brand communication towards a deliriously profitable out-come, and the realities of the limitations of the marketer's control over these things. In particular, because of the internal arrangements of many companies and the strength of many retailers, people called marketing directors are sometimes in reality little more than advertising managers, having relatively little power over those matters that are theoretically their responsibility, other than advertising. This means that they can be in the highly disagreeable position of having more responsibility than power; and equally that they will concern themselves disproportionately with what is supposed to be just one aspect of the job: communication generally and advertising specifically.

If this means that they interest themselves greatly in advertising, it is not perhaps particularly unreasonable. It is after all *their* advertising, in so far as they employ the agency to produce advertising on their behalf for their brand; and ultimately they bear responsibility for anything that goes wrong. If marketers have responsibility without power, agencies are generally in the more attractive position of having power without responsibility. It follows that it is in the agency's own interest to involve their clients in the business of producing advertising to a rather greater extent than is typically the case. For marketers the advertising matters – matters vitally – and they have strong views on it. Agency policy – quite commonplace – of limiting the contact between agency and client to account handlers therefore ensures that marketing people are likely to feel divorced from the *process* of producing advertising and therefore divorced from the product itself: the ads. That way rejection lies. By involving clients – and involving clients particularly with creative people – they can be given the degree of ownership of a creative property that paves the way for its approval. Advertisers are often sufficiently sceptical about account handlers' understanding of their communication problem, let alone that of the creative department. There is no better way of producing good work than ensuring that the creatives genuinely do understand the client's problem and that the advertiser genuinely realises that that is the case.

Getting it out

Whether courtesy of this understanding or not, work of one sort or another will eventually be contrived by the creative department. It is at this point that the full force of the agency's account management swings into action, determined to sell the creative product. In certain respects this is energy misapplied. Account people are gifted sellers, imaginative at dreaming up reasons why work of any nature fits their client's bill. There is sometimes something rather admirable in this inclination – very easily observable – to rise to the challenge of selling what is frequently unsellable. Still, in the end it's unwise. Time and trouble might be better spent in ensuring that the work presented is actually right rather than actually sold. Persuading clients to approve work that the agency collectively realises is indifferent or wrong doesn't solve a problem. It merely delays its manifestation. Sooner or later the work will be found out. Agencies are, of course, constantly under pressure to get on with the next job, to meet copy deadlines etc., etc. The work does have to be got out. Nevertheless the balance between getting the work out and getting it right sometimes seems to favour the former rather at the expense of the latter.

Feedback

In the sort of quasi-scientific diagrams of the advertising process of which agencies are so fond, there is one that is familiar the world over which takes the form of a circle. The student is invited to start at the point labelled 'client brief', follow the procedure through the development of advertising strategy and creative work to the final production of the creativity, the evaluation of the work feeding back into the brief, thus completing the virtuous circle. The

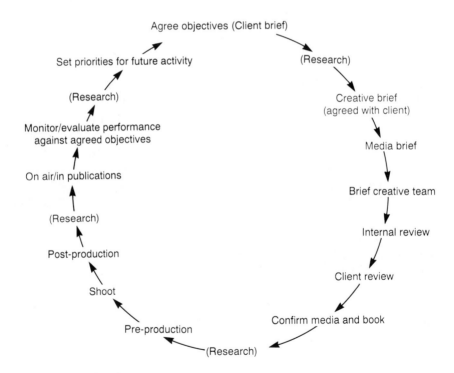

Figure 12.1 The advertising continuum

suggestion, of course, is that the learning garnered as a consequence of the evaluation of the initial work will be fed back into the agency, and the creativity subsequently improved by taking these lessons into account. Of course, while it is not quite fair to say that this never occurs, it's entirely reasonable to suggest it doesn't happen as much as it should. As chapter 10 suggested, the very difficulty of evaluating advertising seems to have ensured that the traditions of concealing any information on the effect of the work from the creative department has been admirably sustained. While understandable, this is still regrettable. It is an arrangement which ensures that the experience of testing an advertisement or a campaign is neglected, that no opportunity can be taken to improve it, that mistakes are perpetuated and perhaps established as features of a campaign, ultimately – as J. Walter Thompson's Jeremy Bullmore has entertainingly suggested in *Behind the Scenes in Advertising* – deified as touch-stones with which one meddles at one's peril.

In the same way as agencies are increasingly being called to account for impact on their work, so too must those immediately responsible for it surely take more seriously the empirical approach to advertising, which ensures that the work can be improved if the nature of the mistakes it makes is known.

Clients are human beings (too)

Many advertising people find dealing with their clients an intermittently – sometimes continually – frustrating process, seeing them as barriers to the production of something that is in fact in their own interests – effective advertising. This leads to a situation in which the client gradually becomes the equivalent of a childhood ogre, a monster and tyrant inaccessible to reason or common sense. Contrary to popular belief, close study indicates that though such cases do certainly exist, they are the exception rather than the rule. The paradox is that clients may appear to be ogres because they – like advertising people – are human too.

While they, their marketing department and their business are theoretically devoted to exemplary marketing and the best possible practices in communication and advertising, their lives and their organisations are all too fallible and human. Notoriously, theirs is an organisation ruled by fear in which experiment is shunned and imagination smothered at birth. Preferment lies only in the most rigid application of the company's two-volume *Rules of Advertising* (Popgood and Grooly, 1936). Naturally, this is a state of affairs which most marketing departments are anxious to conceal from the 'creative' agency hired by the Paris office to ginger up the advertising. So too is the fact that the marketing director is sleeping with the sales director and that the company's balance of power has been hideously compromised. Couple this with the usual frustrations of getting work out of an agency – and a recession – and all is explained. Clients are human too.

BUILDING RELATIONSHIPS

The solution to this situation – if there is one – really does lie in building the relationship between those on both sides of the fence, and establishing the mutual trust and respect that Peter Mead is so keen on. This is something that is very easy to write and say and far less easy to do. It involves:

- a very distinct and conscious effort *on both sides* to do so;
- a lot of agency time making genuine efforts to understand the client business problem;
- a lot of time making genuine efforts to understand the client perspective on that problem and the envisaged solution, if there is one;
- time spent understanding individual client perspectives on the problem – they often differ.

Paradoxically the best way of so doing is spending time outside formal meetings discussing such issues. It is usually on these occasions that the truth – as opposed to the company 'line' emerges.

Once this has been done the tricky business is then to deliver – and deliver continually – against what has been established as the real agenda. Only in this way is the trust and respect that does exist between some agencies and their clients blossom into what can genuinely be a mutually profitable – and enjoyable – relationship.

IRRECONCILABLE DIFFERENCES

Despite all this admirable advice, it may well happen that the relationship between advertiser and agency deteriorates. In the same way as it has been quite persuasively suggested that brands have life-cycles, so too does it seem that accounts have life-cycles within agencies. Without quite mimicking the seven ages of man, it is certainly commonplace that after the account is won there's a honeymoon period in which the agency can do no wrong; a subsequent passage in which nagging doubts arise; some sort of con- solidation during which a few of these faults are addressed; and a final débâcle leading to the sack. The only variable seems to be how long the whole process takes. Yet the sense of this process is perhaps debatable. For the reasons already suggested, the relationship is intrinsically difficult and as a consequence intrinsically unstable, and when tempers wear thin it's in certain respects an easy enough decision for an advertiser to call a review. Whether it is the right decision is another issue. Although there are undoubtedly circumstances in which sacking the agency is the best possible decision, if the objective of the change is to achieve better advertising, in many cases a review is a mistake. Accounts change hands too frequently, the review process consumes very considerable amounts of time, energy and money, and the result is by no means invariably what is desired. Advertisers are guaranteed a different team which will produce different advertising with – for a brief period – rather greater enthusiasm. You are certainly not guaranteed *better* advertising.

Agencies of course – like their clients – quite frequently make mistakes. Advertising is an intrinsically speculative business in that it concerns itself with attempting to influence behaviour in a manner that can't effectively be predicted, even though it can with modest efficiency be measured. It follows that it's unreasonable to fire an agency simply because it gets things wrong. Conversely, you might very reasonably object to one which denied it was wrong in the first place and as a consequence refused to learn from its mistakes. If an agency persistently behaves in such a way then the case against it is unanswerable and a review can very reasonably be called. Generally, though, this will be the exception. The British politician Michael Heseltine has recounted that he was a sufficiently honest man to admit that in the course of his career he had made mistakes, yet a sufficiently good politician to forget exactly what those little errors were. Agencies generally present themselves comparably by – if not going so far as to admit error – at least acknowledging that the work is capable of improvement. Providing such an attitude is evinced, the only legitimate question remaining for a client is whether the agency is capable of delivering – and delivering reasonably promptly – against this brief. It is here sometimes that advertisers mismanage agencies by inappropriately using, or indeed not using, their power.

Agencies generally are very reluctant to lose clients and will go to considerable lengths to retain them if they are aware that the account is unstable. This is reasonable enough in so far as most agencies are, relatively speaking, small businesses and, as has been suggested, losing an account matters – in terms of revenue and in terms of prestige. The problem then lies in the area of communication between the two companies, because all too often agencies are insufficiently clearly aware of precisely how they're regarded by clients; and in particular those in power in agencies are insufficiently clearly aware. This is a pity because clients do have a great deal of power over agencies, and if the right person is familiar with the nature and gravity of the problem, it is more likely that something effective can be done to improve the situation before the relationship reaches the point of no return.

This argues for better communication between agencies and their clients at very senior levels. That this communication doesn't take place very often is a puzzle. Bearing in mind the sorts of money involved and the public nature of the advertising product, you would have thought that the companies would be keen to establish close relationships with agencies. Possibly senior clients find senior agency personnel disagreeable. Perhaps vice versa. Often agencies keen to establish such relationships are rebuffed. This really doesn't help the great advertising cause.

A substitute of sorts is a regular reporting system such as quarterly written reviews of the agency's performance, a format for which appears below. Where such procedures are in place there is a tendency for problems to be recognised by agencies rather earlier than is otherwise the case, and sometimes rectified. It is also highly desirable for agencies to have the facility of formally commenting on client staff. What normally happens, of course, is that some minor irritation on the client's part, unexpressed, grows out of all proportion to the original sin. And at the same time the agency position that the customer is always right delays comment on any problems on the client side. The result is a gradual deterioration in the relationship until suddenly it has reached the point of no return. It's at this stage so easy to call a review. Managing the agency on a day-by-day basis – managing the client on a day-by-day basis – and establishing respect and trust on a firm footing is a far more difficult process. But it may in the end produce better work.

The likelihood nevertheless remains that the cycle which begun so agreeably with a tramp around a few ad agencies, a glance at a few reels, and at least four sumptuous lunches, will now begin again.

AN AGENCY ASSESSMENT PLAN

Section 1 General top management

1 Knowledge/understanding?
   Company · Our business · each assigned brand

2 Attitudes?
   Commitment to the account · Evidence of interest beyond immediate demands of the account?

3 People/competence/talent
Stimulating/challenging · Good to work with?

4 Availability/contact
Access · Positive efforts to maintain contact? · Cover

Section 2 Account management

1 Account director
Competent? · Stimulating to work with? · Committed to development of brand/business · or simply defending the account? · Good at managing and motivating the account team?

2 Account team
All understand the business? · All contribute to the business? · Firm grasp of brand/business strategy and its development? · Do they work well with our strategy framework? · Do they produce good internal briefs for creative department, and control the function well? · Do they produce good internal briefs for media department, and control the function well? · Available when required? · Efficient in terms of administration, progress meetings, contact reports, costings, budget procedures? · Good working client/ agency relationship?

3 Account planners
Proactive (new insights) or do they work narrowly to our brief? · Good at working with research, responding to its findings and making changes as appropriate?

Section 3 Creative

1 Creative director
Accessible when required? · How closely does he/she work on our business? · Sufficient resources always devoted to our business?

2 Creative team
Accessible when required? · All understand the business? · All contribute to the business? · Talent

3 Creativity/creative recommendations (by brand)
Quality/campaignability of core creative idea · Imaginative and innovative performance overall? · On strategy? · On time? · Right first time · or a struggle? · Is creativity for non-TV media at a high standard?

4 Creative work
Administered efficiently to timetables? · Produced within cost constraints?

Section 4 Production

1 Adherence to company guidelines
Competitive quotes obtained? · Liaison with cost consultant? · Provision of cost reconciliations following TV shoots?

2 Does agency production department achieve a good end result?

3 Is production cost-efficient (in relation to production values and market spend norms)?

Section 5 Media

1 Media director
Sufficient contact?

2 Media service
Broad service on media generally · or confined to the specific business/brand?

3 Media planning (by brand)
Competent? · Imaginative? · Thorough?

4 Performance monitoring
Effectiveness/efficiency? · Are plans changed where necessary?

5 Relationships

Section 6 General review

1 Overall summary

2 Better or worse than last year?

3 Is this agency suitable to the brands assigned to it?

4 Could it handle other projects/assignments?

5 Overall performance score

CHECKLIST

1 **The relationship between a client and its agency is intrinsically difficult, yet its maintenance is vital in the production of effective advertising.**

2 **Much in the attitudes and behaviour of those on both sides of the fence compromises this relationship.**

3 Advertisers can help by briefing their agencies more fully and on a more continuous basis, by respecting such expertise as they possess, by better understanding the motives of agency people, and by simplifying approval procedures.

4 Agencies can help by making greater efforts to understand their clients' businesses, involving them to a greater extent in the advertising process, being more critical about the work they sell, and providing better feedback about the impact of the work.

5 If the client–agency relationship breaks down it is partly because it's an intrinsically difficult one, and partly because communications between the parties are poor. Changing agencies is the easy solution to this problem rather than always the right one. Agency–client exchange of views and opinions needs to be improved.

EPILOGUE:
ADVERTISING ON TRIAL
A manifesto for the 1990s

I think it's time we all took a close look at ourselves. Somewhere along the line everything got serious. Somewhere along the line the bottom line became more important than the work that was being turned out. Somewhere along the line everyone in this business got scared at the same time.

The advertising business is failing these days because we're all so afraid to fail. The advertising business isn't fun anymore because we're all so afraid to have fun and get paid for it. The industry has priced itself into a corner. It's time we took a long hard look at our system of compensation. As an industry, we're offering our clients services they don't want and don't need. We've forgotten what we do best is the great ads and the great commercials they do need – work that will help sell people's products and get the country moving. When we get back to doing this, we'll get the business back on its feet.

JERRY DELLA FEMINA
Advertising Age

Advertising in crisis · neglect of the consumer · consumer in flux · integrated marketing · what advertising isn't · what advertising is · need to experiment · motivation to do so · unavoidable success

While it is easy to make generalisations and difficult to be entirely – perhaps at all – accurate about a worldwide business in certain respects as multifarious as advertising, no industry in the throes of its worst recession for a generation, and which has sacked a tenth of its workforce, can be regarded as much other than being in crisis. Its problems of the moment will doubtless be partly dispelled as – so economists promise – the world recession eases as 1994 or 1995 approaches. Yet its troubles are surely more deep-seated.

Of course, like the theatre or the making of a film, advertising is a collective work of art, so at the least the industry hasn't only itself to blame: it has its clients too. And it is the conspiracy between these two partners that ensures that the first thing – surely? – that's wrong with advertising is that it neglects the very people it is supposed to address: the consumer. There is a certain irony here. Marketing as a business philosophy really has been put into effect – at least in a limited way – over the past twenty years and, at least in free markets, it works. Given the option to exercise choice, consumers are very likely to buy the product that best meets their needs. True, the need may not have been realised, acknowledged or articulated before the product was launched to meet it – think of the Sony Walkman – but generally manufacturers who give people what they want, rather than what it is convenient for them to produce, are the ones who succeed. Now it might be imagined that of all disciplines within a company, marketing would there-fore be the strongest advocate of the consumer. Equally, that of all industries, advertising, the public face of marketing, might not so much follow suit but lead the way in championing the shopper's rights. The fact is that often this isn't so. Marketing departments and agencies pay lip-service to the people the advertising addresses and little more. And this is the fount and origin of the problems that the advertising business faces as – of all things – a new millenium approaches.

The principle presumably is that ignorance is bliss. Certainly, many concerned seem remarkably happy with surprisingly superficial notions of who buys their brand, where they buy it, how often and why they buy it, who's buying it less, who's buying it more, how they might be influenced – especially by advertising – into buying more; how the advertising that is there affects what they're currently doing. In so far as brands matter in the larger scheme of things – arguably a question in itself – these things matter. It is on consumer behaviour that sales of the brand depend. And if their behaviour – perversely – can't be controlled by marketers, it can at least be influenced. Consumer behaviour – consumer sentiment – matters. Appre-ciating this point and doing something about it really does seem to involve a quite radical change in the way the marketing and advertising process is thought about, organised and managed. At the moment, advertising is really a game for two players: the advertiser and the agency. The agency has a view on what the advertising should be like: the advertiser disagrees; and the result is a compromise normally in the shape of a camel. In the more sophisticated alliances one partner occasionally justifies, or more likely post-rationalises, a decision by reference to the consumer. That's about all. The sooner advertisers and their agencies adapt to including the consumer in the equation, the better off in every sense they will surely be.

This is a challenge. It doesn't happen at the moment and it will be difficult to make it happen because it means both agency and advertiser ceding a degree of power to a third party: the form the advertising takes will depend on how it affects consumers rather than just what the advertiser and the agency think about it. Agencies and their clients both like power, and consumers are non-entities. Equally it is a problem because both parties really don't manage the collection, analysis, dissemination and, above all, use of information about the consumer very well. Of course, in many respects, the ultimate provider of this information, the market research industry, is here to blame, itself paradoxically careless of the needs of its customers. Many market and marketing researchers are genuinely gifted at collecting information from and about consumers. Fewer are good at presenting this material to those who use the information, and fewer still manifest sufficient understanding of the meaning of the information. Or, at least, the meaning of the information to the marketer. This discourages marketing people who – generally – are busy people trying to make practical decisions in a hurry. The presentation, particularly of quantitative information, seems sometimes designed less to illuminate than to obscure. The other contributory factor is the lowly status – both within agencies and client companies – of market research departments. The world naturally accords status to doers above thinkers, but whether it should do this is another matter. The way ahead in marketing – as perhaps in one or two other fields – surely lies in the closer conjunction of thinking and doing than the internal arrangements of most institutions and companies – politically, socially, culturally, even geographically – permits. Research – marketing intelligence is perhaps a more positive and accurate phrasing – needs to be a far more integral part of the marketing and advertising process.

This is only the beginning of what should surely be a five-year plan. If the business is to act upon rather than – as hitherto – merely state the idea that the customer is king, then it also has to acknowledge that the monarchy is in a constant state of flux. It is vital to know who a brand's customers are, what they buy, when they buy, why they buy etc., but it is equally important to appreciate that the answer to this question in most markets is one that is constantly changing. It is obviously not true that the same people go on buying the same brand, at the same place, at the same level of frequency *ad infinitum*. Apart from anything else, they die. It is not even true that the same sort of people go on buying the same brand, from the same place, at the same frequency. Brand profiles change continuously and in growing markets they can change rapidly.

Like the general point about the importance of the consumer, this notion of change matters. Brand management can be defined in various ways, but perhaps its essence may be regarded as the anticipation of, and adaptation to, changing market circumstances. This seems obvious enough, but in fact it isn't practised as much as it might be. Many brands react to circumstances long after they might reasonably have been anticipated. Brand management is essentially a reactive rather than a proactive discipline, and much the same could be said of the advertising that goes with it. Agencies sometimes seem to appreciate insufficiently that the markets they work in, and the consumers within them, are movable feasts. That they are is clear enough. The corollary is that in the majority of market circumstances the brand too *has* to be in a state of constant evolution if it is not to be overtaken by events. Most brands must run simply to stand still, and must sprint to out-perform the market. Two things then follow. If the essence of marketing intelligence is about understanding the consumer, its essence is also about appreciating and evaluating the constant change, not only of the people who buy a brand, but also the other market circumstances that impact upon sales – like price, distribution and competitive activity. Change – or at least monitoring and preferably anticipating that change – is all. As Carl Spielvogel of the Saatchi-owned agency Backer Spielvogel Bates remarks: 'Our business is to help our clients, by whatever means, with the orderly management of change in the market-place.'

The second point is that something has to be done about this notion of change. As ever in marketing this is difficult. Product development and brand extension tend to be regarded as activities isolated from the day-to-day management of a brand. The reality is that nothing should be further from the truth. Brand management in most cases *is* brand development and those brands that survive are indeed those that constantly change to adapt to changing market conditions. And this means change by changing – or at least evolving – such things as product formulation, packaging, positioning and advertising to meet the new circumstances. Reluctance to tamper with a proven formula is understandable. But a formula that works well one year is virtually by definition one that will work less well the next. The marketers' motto has to be 'change and survive'.

Bringing the consumer into the picture and appreciating the constancy with which consumers change are therefore the starting-points of the revolution in advertising practice that the business needs. However, that in itself isn't quite enough.

Now in advertising it is the advertising message about the brand and the means of its expression that centrally concern advertisers and their agencies, and – centrally – shouldn't. They shouldn't because this isn't the way in which the shopper sees the brand: it merely reflects the idiosyncratic organisation of the marketing process. Consumers see brands in a way marketers rarely do: as a whole. They have a genuine need: they go to a shop to try to meet that need; they ask retailers their recommendations; they inspect the various brands; they notice such issues as price; they use their own money to buy them; and then they consume, employ, use, read, drink, devour or digest as the instructions dictate. They may then even see some advertising. This is a time-consuming business involving a series of separate exercises and decision-making processes. Nevertheless, it is the reality of people buying brands.

The consequence of this is that there is a certain need to see brands as the consumer sees them: steadily and whole. If the business did do that to a slightly greater extent, it might more readily appreciate the holistic nature of marketing and act accordingly. This means quite simply that if brand management is all about continuously evolving a brand's meaning to meet changing market circumstances, then the key to the implementation of this process lies not in getting the direct mail, packaging or advertising right, but in the co-ordination of these things to produce a united front for the brand. It would be naïve to say this was easy. Yet it is nevertheless a necessity. Or rather, the force of the logic of integrated marketing is such that it is tempting to imagine that it will be the exception rather than the rule in twenty-first century marketing. The obstacle to its implementation is of course organisational and political rather than intellectual. No one really thinks it is a bad idea. The problem lies more in the fact that suppliers – say, of good packaging – are rarely equally good suppliers of good advertising. And then that one communication supplier is loath to develop for its particular discipline an idea created for another. Hence the impasse. The reality though is that communication suppliers are beginning to work together and seem likely to have to do so rather more closely in the future if they are to survive. In certain respects unfortunately, advertisers increasingly realise that total communications marketing makes sense. The consequence of all this is that what the advertising says and how it says it do have to be related to a greater extent than hitherto with the other forms of communication activity that feature on virtually every single brand. The whole is indeed greater than the sum of the parts, and certainly greater than the sum of the advertising.

This isn't to say that what the advertising says and how it says it are irrelevant. Rather, that they are only relevant in the context of other activity – to which they may indeed be catalytic. In this context what can loosely be called advertising strategy matters a great deal, using the phrase not to mean how the ads will achieve their goals, but what in the first case those goals are.

It is often here, of course, that misunderstandings between advertiser and agency arise. What is advertising? Why advertise? Does advertising work? How does it work? When does it stop working? Who makes it work? How can I get advertising that works better? The one certainty about these questions is that an advertiser and its agency will give different answers to each and every one. Given the position in which they sit this is perhaps inevitable, but progress might be made if there was a more concerted effort made by various associations of advertisers and the various associations of agencies to find – or at least enlarge the areas of – common ground.

As a starting-point it is merely necessary to exaggerate by suggesting that whereas agencies see advertising as an end in itself, advertisers see their campaigns as a means to an end of sales, and both are wrong. The argument then goes that this is where the debilitating trouble between client and agency really stems from, and that reconciliation and compromise between the two parties might bear fruit presumably agreeable to both by way of better advertising. This is to say that if the two sides agreed what they were making, then a greater degree of satisfaction with the final product might result. Inevitably this could be provocative, indeed rash. What is advertising if it is not (a) an end itself and (b) a means to the end of sales? What indeed?

The answer, of course, is that advertising is a means to an end rather than an end itself, but the end that it seeks is not sales. Advertising is a form of expression which employs conventional ways in which people express themselves, such as words, pictures, drama, movement and music. In this sense it is quite simply an art form and is perfectly reasonably regarded as one of the arts – if not necessarily quite fine art. Equally, it is not simply an art. Advertising is a form of expression but it's further defined by restricting itself – generally – in what it expresses to what the advertiser wishes the consumer to buy. In this sense it is correctly defined as it used to be, as a branch of commercial art. Its subject-matter is – broadly speaking – brands; its method of expression designed not to *say* something about those brands but to *communicate* something: to make people understand and remember what is said. Therein lies the art. Now this, of course, divorces advertising both from the idea that it is an end in itself and that its end is sales. Advertising is the business of influencing what consumers think and feel about brands. Along with other factors, this influences sales.

Now this all seems simple enough, and indeed there are probably relatively few marketing or advertising people who would find such a definition contentious. Nevertheless, the definition does have crucial consequences for how advertising is created, which are sometimes ignored. These are that advertising seems sometimes to be produced for the purposes of self-expression, and that advertising should have a direct and measurable sales effect. Yet, given the definition, neither is true. If advertising is about influencing what people feel about brands, then it must be produced with an eye to what its consumers, rather than its creators, feel. And if advertising is about influencing what people feel about brands then it should be measured as such. Neither is quite as commonplace as might be hoped.

The only issue then to be settled is how this is all to be achieved. Perhaps in many respects it is fortunate that this remains stubbornly unknown. There *are* those who, for their own ends, attempt to sway public opinion – Marx, Stalin, Franco, Mussolini, Hitler, Tito, Ceauşescu, Thatcher and the like. But – as history teaches us – all are in the end undone. The lesson here lies in the very unpredictability and volatility of public opinion. Ideas that a hundred years ago seemed unalterably fixed in the firmament – the superiority of the white over the black races, that of men over women, Coke over Pepsi, Great Britain over the rest of the world – are now derided. So too with the things that engender, nurture, mature and ultimately destroy ideas. Who, on the one hand, would have predicted the influence of Marx? Or, on the other, the movement's extraordinary collapse? What creates cultures like nationalism, feminism, ageism and sexism? How do they begin and end? These may be large issues, but they too are matters of public sentiment. The fact is that we don't know, and cannot with any certainty predict, what will capture the public's imagination either by way of national movements or ads for Coke. There, in many respects, lies the fascination of the historical process; and in many respects also the fascination of advertising.

Now, that unpredictability is important as a principle because of the growing pressures to make advertising accountable. It is entirely under-standable that advertisers wish to know that if they invest a certain sum in advertising a brand then a certain return may be expected – if not guaranteed. The unpredictability of public opinion means very simply that it can't. And not only can we not predict the impact of a campaign on the public, also we never will. Or at least while humans remain humans we won't. We will, with increasing accuracy, be able to say what the advertising has done and even, to an extent, how it has done it. Better targeting and better strategies, and better media placement will incrementally improve the advertising product, but the linchpin will remain the creativity, and it seems unlikely that it will ever be possible to say definitively whether or how well this will work. In the context of the pressures for advertising accountability, little could be more important. Advertising is a business that is in many respects rightly under scrutiny. It has done things it ought not to have done and has left undone many that it should. Still, it remains the chief channel of communication between producer and purchaser, and if it is to continue to prosper it is going to have to mount a concerted rearguard action against the daily growing forces of those who make money by attempting to predict the unpredictable. These forces are among the various threats to the industry and a significant barrier to improving the quality of the advertising. The problem is that the need to predict has never been greater and will continue to grow. However, the impact of advertising is intrinsically unpredictable and the established measures to predict it, if anything, militate against the impact of the work.

If, then, the temptation to predict has to be avoided, just the opposite is the case when assessing the work after it has run. It is just possible to imagine that there is quite a lot of work to be done in this area, especially in the context of advertising that isn't intended to elicit a direct and immediate response: the expensive, long-term brand-building work which is the industry's – and its clients' – life-blood. The truth is that even in countries which regard their advertising industries as sophisticated, in far fewer cases than one might hope is any serious, concerted, long-term attempt made to discover in the first instance *if* the advertising has worked at all; and within that minority in only a smaller minority is there debate of a sophisticated sort as to how it's working and, even, how it might work better. This is partly because these questions aren't terribly easy to answer, but it is also because it is easier not to bother to answer them. Yet, in due course, it is undoubtedly in everyone's interest to do just that. Some advertising certainly works better than other advertising, some works a great deal better, and the agency that can prove beyond reasonable doubt that its advertising was doing an excellent job would have a very good case to be paid by these results and to attract more business accordingly. Those agencies that succeed in the next century will presumably be those in the vanguard of proving – or at least making a better case for – their advertising's effectiveness. Advertisers will be increasingly reluctant to assume that the advertising works and that the agency can be trusted to produce such work. They will want to know that it works, know how well it works, and know that the agency is trying to make it work better. As things stand, advertising is still very much a matter of faith in what it is – generally – the assumption that the advertising is working and – sometimes – not. In the majority of cases it will perhaps never be possible to prove that the ads have worked. It is not only possible but also absolutely necessary to improve the grounds for that belief, and therefore trying to adopt a more empirical approach to the whole advertising business: trying something and seeing if it works, rather than – as at present – trying something.

Now this all pleads for a commitment from agencies not only to improve their handling of the component parts of the advertising process, but also to begin to think of advertising in what for some seems a new way: as a means of producing a measurable effect on the consumer, not as an end in itself. This means changing or at least evolving the philosophy towards its product, but it also means evolving its relationship with its clients. The relationship between agencies and their clients is often poor, indeed in many respects it is counter-productive to what it is supposed to be the joint task of producing –

or improving the quality of – the advertising. Of course, both sides are to blame, but of the two the agency side is certainly the most reprehensible. And, all too often, agencies treat their clients badly.

'Business partnership' is a phrase much mouthed by agencies, but sometimes little they do in practice nurtures such a relationship. The bottom line is that some agencies, while purporting to be working on behalf of their clients, actually regard them as prey. As slow on their feet as in thought, advertisers and their budgets are fair game for fast-moving, quick-footed, light-fingered ad-men, who often seem to see advertisers more as people to exploit than to serve. This is of course manifested generally in what some see as a whiff of irresponsibility in the industry towards the effectiveness of its product, and specifically in profiteering on third-party costs. While such attitudes and practices prevail, and are known to prevail both by advertisers and within the industry itself, talk of partnership might be thought of as hypocrisy. The irony of course is that these things are entertainingly self-defeating. There is no doubt that advertising works – or some of it anyway – there's little doubt that the need for advertising to launch and differentiate products and brands will continue into the next century, and there's equally little doubt that marketers are reasonably aware of the value of advertising – or at least good advertising. The opportunities for the industry are therefore considerable and the opportunity for responsible practitioners greater. Yet, at the moment, there sometimes doesn't seem to be sufficient inclination to take advantage of them. Advertisers by and large believe that advertising works and will pay for advertising that works. The industry is guardian of a technique, a property, a means of expression the value of which it seems sometimes scarcely to appreciate: the Sèvres vase - perhaps – in the hands of the PG Tips chimpanzee. That this will change is surely inevitable. The question is rather how quickly it will change and who – which particular agencies and which particular countries – will benefit most from this change. The beneficiaries will, of course, be those who change most rapidly towards a situation in which the agency regards its clients' competitors as prey, rather the clients themselves.

One of the keys to such changes undoubtedly lies in reviewing the ways in which agencies are remunerated. The historical arrangement was very simply that advertisers bought advertising by the yard – more recently the metre – and the agency was rewarded on that basis: a percentage of media bought. The result of this was entirely predictable: that agencies produced advertising by the yard. The difficulty is merely that, on the whole, advertising isn't a commodity and isn't best produced on this basis. Any arrangement whereby agencies are paid not according to how much advertising they produce, but by how much of it works, is thus a considerable improvement.

It provides agencies with the only incentive they really understand to create advertising that works. Paying them to produce advertising means that they'll produce advertising. Paying them to produce advertising that works may not produce advertising that works, but on balance, taking all things into account, it does seem more likely to.

In passing, it might be remarked here that this does imply a certain emphasis on the part of agencies towards the profit motive. This is a feature of the industry which is becoming more rather than less marked. Of course, if financial success was directly related to the quality of the advertising produced, this wouldn't be so much reasonable as admirable. Still, at the moment this isn't the case, and the stress on turnover and margins may be more regrettable. Advertising is a business and businesses are in business to make money. Still, it is possible to wonder again here whether means aren't rather being confused with ends, which is to say that traditional thinking might suggest that agencies make money so as to produce advertising, rather than making advertising so as to produce money. Clearly, this is a matter of degree not kind. But the impression of some within advertising these days is certainly that the cart has run away with the horse. Agencies have to remain profitable to stay in business and they've got to be really quite profitable to retain the talent they require to take them into the next century. They need nevertheless to retain the balance between profitability and – loosely speaking – creativity. The heart of the agency should lie in the business of making advertising rather than the business of making money, and one of the various reasons why the standard of advertising has slipped in the past four years – and slipped it has – is that agencies have concerned themselves more with making money than making advertising.

This, finally, raises the issue of motivation and the relationship between advertisers and agencies from which it stems: the ultimate key to better advertising. As one leading advertiser quoted in *Campaign* remarked: 'We want better strategies, better targeting, better creativity, better media placement, better thinking. We aim to ensure we get agencies' best people on our business and then ensure they are motivated to work their butts off, producing outstanding work for us.' This summarises the argument. Agencies do indeed need to produce better targeting, creativity, media placement and thinking. The management issue is then how to ensure that the agency really does work its butt off.

This is awkward. As has been suggested, one of the defining characteristics of the production of advertising is that it is a peculiarly collective act. A campaign – even an individual execution – represents the thinking of the various agency disciplines, combined with those on the client side. Assuming the competence of all concerned – sometimes a dangerous thing –

assuming a willingness to produce solutions unique to the given advertising problem rather than a reflex response – also dangerous – then the central problem is one of motivating groups of people normally with very different sorts of talent and personality, and normally quite busy too, to do just that.

At the moment, a sufficiently bad job of this is done to ensure that most advertising is – to take a figure borne of experience – perhaps half as good as it could be. This seems mildly regrettable. The truth is, of course, that agencies the world over provide minimal training in man-management in a business that, ironically, is definable and defined as a people business. Equally, while advertisers are normally rather more diligent in such matters, few provide specific help for their managers on the genuinely demanding task of running agencies. And agencies are difficult for clients, as well as their executives, to run. They are ambitious, money-grabbing, temperamental, egotistical and manipulative; while at the same time being producers of invaluable material. If agencies can be, and often are, sacked, so too can, and do, agencies sack their clients and get individuals sacked within them. Agencies wield power. Account management within agencies and their clients outside both need help. If this situation patently hadn't obtained for so long, it would be fair to assume that it couldn't continue much longer. In the circumstances it is still difficult to believe that the situation won't improve simply because it is so much in everyone's interest for it to do so. Currently, advertisers normally obtain very far from the best they can from agencies. It is up to all concerned that they obtain something approaching slightly closer to the best.

How, then, do you get better advertising? Advertising about taking risks – creative risks in trying to see what really will influence public opinion. In many countries over the last three years nothing has been more inimical than taking risks. The result has been very simple. The quality of advertising, the return on advertising has declined. The solution involves reorientating the whole marketing and advertising process towards something to which the business merely pays lip-service, namely the consumer; it means acknowledging that the consumer is in a state of constant change and that the consumer, unlike the marketer, sees the brand steadily and sees it whole; it means that greater attention has to be paid to the sum of the brand communication parts; it means that agencies have to be better managed and better motivated, partly through paying them by results. And it means a new approach to advertising that is definable as the empirical approach. This is the approach that acknowledges how difficult it is to predict consumers' reponse to advertising, works hard to lessen the odds by the careful setting of objectives etc., but then concentrates far more than is currently the case on finding out how consumers really are responding to the work.

By following this simple prescription, the reader is surely bound to find success 'practically unavoidable'.

INDEX